Putting Your *Past* Behind You

Putting Your *Past* Behind You

Finding Hope for Life's Deepest Hurts

ERWIN W. LUTZER

MOODY PUBLISHERS
CHICAGO

Edited by Kevin Mungons
Interior design: Ragont Design
Cover design: Studio Gearbox
Cover photo of leaf copyright © 2024 by Popovo Bros/Shutterstock (2048967053). All rights reserved.

Library of Congress Cataloging-in-Publication Data

Names: Lutzer, Erwin W. author
Title: Putting your past behind you : finding hope for life's deepest hurts
    / Erwin W. Lutzer.
Description: Chicago : Moody Publishers, [2025] | "Originally published by
    Here's Life Publishers, © 1990"--Title page verso. | Includes
    bibliographical references. | Summary: "Lutzer shows how to break from
    our past. People have experienced the same trials, addictions, and
    injustices as you. Many have traveled beyond the pain to become blessed
    servants of Christ. God is ready to help, and He uses His people to
    share in His work of restoration and healing"-- Provided by publisher.
Identifiers: LCCN 2024049448 (print) | LCCN 2024049449 (ebook) | ISBN
    9780802436221 paperback | ISBN 9780802468673 ebook
Subjects: LCSH: Christian life | Spiritual healing | Consolation
Classification: LCC BV4501.3 .L8645 2025 (print) | LCC BV4501.3 (ebook) |
    DDC 248.4--dc23/eng
LC record available at https://lccn.loc.gov/2024049448
LC ebook record available at https://lccn.loc.gov/2024049449

Originally delivered by fleets of horse-drawn wagons, the affordable paperbacks from D. L. Moody's publishing house resourced the church and served everyday people. Now, after more than 125 years of publishing and ministry, Moody Publishers' mission remains the same—even if our delivery systems have changed a bit. For more information on other books (and resources) created from a biblical perspective, go to www.moodypublishers.com or write to:

Moody Publishers
820 N. LaSalle Boulevard
Chicago, IL 60610

1 3 5 7 9 10 8 6 4 2

Printed in the United States of America

To all who seek to believe that
the grace in God's heart is greater than the pain in their past

Contents

Introduction

Thousands of people live with the fear that their past will return to haunt them. And even if their secret should never come to light, it invades the mind to torment them, to defeat them, and remind them that they have disappointed God and themselves. Every time they take a step forward, they feel as if they must drag a ball-and-chain with them.

The fragmentation of the family and the widespread loss of values has transformed us into a heartless culture bent on self-fulfillment at any cost. Little wonder many people have a past characterized by betrayal, abuse, and a litany of destructive decisions.

This book is based on the conviction that ultimately only Christ can enable us to put our past behind us. I do not mean that the impact of our past is obliterated, for we will always carry with us the sum total of our experiences. But our past need not cripple our walk with God. Indeed, it can be the motivation we need to pursue God more fervently.

God does not always free us from all the effects of the past, but its power can be broken. Indeed, it is often in the lives of those who have suffered most keenly that God does His deepest work. Thousands can testify that God does make us whole if we give Him all the pieces, as seen in this poem by Faith L. Mischler:

As children bring their broken toys,
  With tears for us to mend,
I brought my broken dreams to God
  Because He was my friend.

But then instead of leaving Him
  In peace to work alone,
I hung around and tried to help
  With ways that were my own.

At last, I snatched them back and cried,
  "How can you be so slow?"
"My child," He said, "What could I do?
  "You never did let go."[1]

Let us now embark on a journey that will enable us to find God in our past and build a better future.

Chapter 1

Living with a Tattoo

When I asked a woman about the tattoo on her arm, she explained, "My former boyfriend did it—he was an abusive alcoholic." She was now happily married to another man, but every day she was reminded of the pain in her past. She would have preferred to remove that tattoo, but it was burned into her skin.

We've all met people whose past is tattooed onto their souls. They've experienced abuse, lived in immorality, or acquired addictions. Some are women who live with the memory of an abortion; others are men who have fathered children out of wedlock or ruined their families. I heard a news report of a young woman who turned her own father over to the authorities because she had seen him commit a murder when she was a child. Think of the memories tattooed onto her soul!

"I'm trying to rebuild my life, like a house that has been destroyed within and without," a woman wrote after she heard one of our radio broadcasts. "I hope to rebuild from the ground floor, and, if possible, not use any of the rotten wood I find all around me. This time, I hope to do the maintenance so that it won't be ruined again."

How different our past would be if we could relive it knowing what we know now. Louisa Fletcher Tarkington expressed the wish of millions when she wrote:

I wish there were some wonderful place
Called the Land of Beginning Again
Where all our mistakes and heartaches
And all of our poor selfish grief
Could be dropped like a shabby old coat at the door
And never put on again.[2]

Is there such a place? I believe there is.

True, we cannot begin again in time, for hours become days, days become months, and months become years that can never be relived. No one can go back to the starting line in the race of life. Tacking an outdated calendar on the wall will not bring back the years, nor allow us to erase imprints left by mistakes of bygone days. We cannot go to God, as one teenager did, with "Lord, I pray this accident might not have happened!"

Like holes left in the wall after nails have been removed, the gaping wounds of sin often leave ugly sores. God wants to bandage our open wounds so that they might be healed. When those wounds have become battle scars, we will know that healing has taken place. Guilt, regret, and bitter heartache can be put behind us—there is a land of beginning again. Our past need not control our present nor future. It is never too late to do what is right; never too late to live our remaining days for God.

In *The Scarlet Letter,* Nathaniel Hawthorne tells the story of a woman who has a love affair with a young minister. As the story opens, she is being punished by having to stand on a public platform with the large letter *A,* for "Adultery," on her breast. She holds her daughter, born out of wedlock. As the scenario unfolds, she makes public expiation for her sin, taking the insults of the townspeople as her due—but she steadfastly refuses to name the father of her child.

In the meantime, her husband, a shrewd psychologist, pretends to befriend the man whom he suspects was the accomplice in the affair.

On the pretext of being a doctor, the woman's husband makes this man squirm for years because the minister will not admit his guilt.

In the story, the immoral man who would not own up to his past suffered far more than the woman who faced her sin, accepting her shame and guilt. Better to come clean than to live with painful secrets that imprison the soul! If the immoral man had been willing to face his past, he could have lived with a clean, forgiven conscience. In choosing to feign innocence, he had to secretly confront his sin every single day.

THE HOPE OF A NEW BEGINNING

In the Old Testament we read the remarkable story of Gomer, a woman who knew only too well what it was like to live with the letter *A* stamped on her soul. Her husband, Hosea, a prophet, had been commanded by God to marry a prostitute. Most Bible scholars believe she was not a harlot when he married her; nevertheless, God did say, "Go, take to yourself a wife of whoredom and have children of whoredom, for the land commits great whoredom by forsaking the LORD" (Hos. 1:2).

Hosea had two children by this woman; but when the third was born, the prophet became painfully aware the child was not his. He named the boy "Lo-ammi," which means "no kin of mine."

Gomer continued her affairs, flitting from one lover to another, never finding the acceptance and fulfillment she craved. One day she fell into the hands of a man who was unable to care for her. Hosea saw her from a distance—distraught, humiliated, without food or clothes. Instinctively, he took some bread and wine and gave it to her slothful lover so he could take better care of his mistress!

Gomer's moral toboggan slide continued until she finally ended up in the hands of a man who had her auctioned off to the highest bidder. Men stood and gawked at this hapless slave whose beauty had long since been marred by the high cost of emotional and spiritual decadence. Hosea outbid the other men and paid the fifteen shekels of silver and a bushel (a "homer") and a half of barley. Was Hosea irrational? What man would make such a painful sacrifice for a wife who had humiliated him, flaunting broken marriage vows and treating her children irresponsibly? Let her sleep in the beds she had made.

Foolish or not, Hosea brought her home, knowing he could now be with his lover again. He believed their marriage still had a future. They would rekindle the love of their courtship.

What had inspired such hope in the prophet? Hosea was convinced that they could begin again. He hoped she had reached bottom, had learned her lessons, and was ready to flee to him and to God. If she was not ready for a new beginning, her future would have died permanently.

God Himself gave Hosea hope when He said,

> Therefore, behold, I will allure her,
> Bring her into the wilderness
> And speak kindly to her.
> Then I will give her vineyards from there,
> And the valley of Achor as a door of hope.
> And she will sing there as in the days of her youth,
> As in the day when she came up from the land of Egypt.
> (Hos. 2:14–15 NASB 1995)

Gomer would sing again.

And there is more to the story. Her marriage vows would be reinstated, and she would live in purity and faithful commitment to her husband.

> I will betroth you to Me forever;
> Yes, I will betroth you to Me in righteousness and in justice,
> In favor and in compassion,
> And I will betroth you to Me in faithfulness.
> Then you will know the LORD.
> (2:19–20 NASB 1995)

Eventually, she would be almost as though she had never sinned. Yes, she would sing again. She would stop her running and come home where she belonged. Spiritually speaking, her virginity would be restored. She could no longer be a virgin physically, but spiritually her virginity was restored; she was a virgin in her heart. God gave her a new beginning.

I'm not saying the book of Hosea was written to give us an example of how a husband should treat a wayward wife—though God only knows how many marriages could be salvaged if the partners determined to show love even in the midst of unfaithfulness. Hosea's marriage does illustrate a point, however. No matter how far someone falls, restoration is always possible. God loves to save great sinners—even those wearing the big *A*.

No matter how deep or dark your valley, there is always a path leading out. God specializes in difficult cases. Anyone can begin again.

PERSPECTIVES FOR A NEW BEGINNING

The church in Corinth was made up of many believers converted out of homosexuality, adultery, drunkenness, and physical abuse. They lived in a culture much like ours, yet even more decadent. Paul wanted to assure them they could have a new beginning, a new life in Christ. In fact, many of them had already experienced it.

He wrote:

No temptation has overtaken you that is not common to man. God is faithful, and he will not let you be tempted beyond your ability, but with the temptation he will also provide the way of escape, that you may be able to endure it. (1 Cor. 10:13)

Here is some good news for those who think their sordid past must control their future. We are not in the struggle alone; God walks with us through our past failures and future temptations. This passage of Scripture gives us perspective.

You Are Not Alone in Your Struggle

Your past—no matter how painful it is to remember—is common to the human race. This does not mean everyone has had your experiences, but that others have come through similar challenges and have done so triumphantly. In fact, Paul would say that the struggles of humanity are quite common. Your own private history has been lived, at least to some degree, by someone else.

Alcoholism
Child abuse
Divorce
Gluttony
Abortion
Homosexuality
Sexual addictions

Many people with one or more of these failures in their past have gone on to become blessed servants of Christ. You can overcome your past, whatever it involves. The purpose of this book is to explain what the Bible has to say about God's role in the process. Others have put a past just like yours behind them; so can you.

If we as a believing church wish to prove Christ's power, we must give credible hope to those whose backgrounds are cluttered with addictions, immorality, and/or criminal behavior. One quarter of all children born this year will, at some time, live with just one parent; others will experience the terror of having an alcoholic father or a dysfunctional mother.[3] Across their lifetime, one in three women are subjected to physical or sexual abuse, usually from a close friend or relative.[4]

These experiences are common to fallen humanity. Some people are greater sinners than others, and some have been sinned against in greater ways, but we all have the same human nature. Every one of us is somewhere on a continuum. To some degree we have all experienced the power of sin and have opened the door to temptation. Or we have felt the sting of being betrayed and used.

If I could listen to your story, it might resemble many of the others I've heard in my lifetime. I would look at you and say that your trial, your addiction, your injustice is common to man. You are not facing your hurt alone. God stands by to help; and He almost always uses His people to share in His work of restoration and healing.

Of course I don't mean to imply that what has happened to you is not serious just because it has happened to others, too. The fact that emotional and spiritual hurt are common does not make them less painful. Nor does it exonerate the person who inflicted the pain. Admitting the depth of that hurt might be the first step toward recovery. What I *am* saying is that *no matter what you are facing, there is someone else in this world who has had the same past as you and has faced it successfully and gone on to live a productive life.*

One of the chains Satan uses to keep people bound to their past is secrecy. They believe their situation is unique, that no one else has lived through their hell. Thus, some who hurt carry within their hearts a dreaded secret, believing that if anyone else knew about what they had done, they themselves would be rejected. Secrecy becomes their spiritual tomb.

As a pastor, I have frequently heard people say, "I'm going to tell you something that no one else in all the world knows." Then follows a tale of abuse, sexual perversion, or cruel injustice. I think to myself, *What a pity this person has had to bear his burden all alone these many years—even though his story is common to man.*

God Is Faithful

"God is faithful, and he will not let you be tempted beyond your ability," wrote Paul in 1 Corinthians 10:13. If I think I am going through a trial that is too much for God, I am calling His credibility into question. God's faithfulness means He is obligated to not give me more than I can handle.

The addict says, "God cannot give me anything that can match the euphoria of psychedelic drugs, illicit sexuality, or alcoholism. He is no competition for the drives that control me, for the power that exhilarates me." Such a person denies God's faithfulness, and thus he remains bound in his sins. The freedom that God gives is better than the euphoria of sins that cloud our conscience and pollute the soul.

Understandably, thousands of people (yes, I am including Christians) are angry with God. After all, the argument goes, if God loved me, why did He let me get into this mess? Why was my father an alcoholic? Why do I have such strong sexual desires? Why did He let my dad abuse me, or my mother reject me? Why should I look to a God who failed me when I needed Him the most?

Thus, the God who can help is held at bay. The very source of strength and understanding that is so needed is rejected. I have never met a person who has successfully overcome a difficult past who has not had to "forgive God." (Although He does not need forgiveness, we sometimes think He does!) A man who was formerly involved in the gay lifestyle told me he never had a partner who wasn't angry with the Almighty. Many in the gay community are angry because they believe this is the way God made them. They believe this is the card they were dealt.

No one can put his past behind him until he resolves this hostility against God. To understand His sovereign control over the world and yet to believe He is loving is difficult. An abused woman put it to me simply, "God wasn't there for me when I was a child; why should I think He will be there for me as an adult? *I can never trust Him!*" Yet trust Him she must if she is to have rest in her soul.

How can such anger be dissolved? We must be honest in expressing to Him exactly how we feel. I've met people who think God would smite them with a lightning bolt if they were to tell Him they feel betrayed by Him. So rather than confront Him, they ignore Him, stuffing their hostility into their souls like garbage into a bag. The smoldering anger is stored away until it becomes unbearable. Some go to their graves in silent but seething bitterness.

David had a better solution. He would pour out his soul to God, openly admitting his disappointments and anger. He did it reverently, of course, but he did it honestly.

> "Will the Lord spurn forever,
> and never again be favorable?
> Has his steadfast love forever ceased?
> Are his promises at an end for all time?
> Has God forgotten to be gracious?
> Has he in anger shut up his compassion?"
> Then I said, "I will appeal to this,
> to the years of the right hand of the Most High."
> (Ps. 77:7–10)

In numerous passages David questions God, asking why He has hidden His face. Then David confesses his confusion and disappointment with his Lord. God did not rebuke him for such honesty; it would have been worse if David had not talked to God at all. The Almighty is well able to take the heat—even if it is not deserved.

Since God knows what we think about Him, why not say it? He will not be surprised! Festering bitterness can be siphoned off only by honest communication. Whenever we are open with God, we will discover that grace has been poured into our souls.

If the first chain that ties us to our past is *secrecy,* the second is *hostility.* Anger toward God and others makes us stay in our own prisons, nursing a heart as hard as stone. It poisons all of our relationships. Yet God is faithful. You can tell Him everything, and He will keep it a secret. The chains of the past can be broken.

God Will Provide

Paul wrote that He will "also provide the way of escape, that you may be able to endure it" (1 Cor. 10:13). To bear raw pain is so excruciating that we all seek some escape route that will make life manageable. By nature we try to dodge our painful past so that we don't have to face it. Initially, this seems like the easiest path, but in the end it is much more difficult. As we shall see, God's way of escape is quite different from ours.

In the next chapter, I will expose the prison called denial. Abuse victims resort to denial to avoid the pain of reality; perpetrators resort to denial to protect their facade of innocence. Children develop happy fantasies to compensate for the hurt of real life. Such denial is common, but it is never a permanent, satisfying way of putting our past behind us.

Denial enables us to convince ourselves that we are in control of our lives, and all is well. Once we start down that road, we will play a hundred manipulative games to get ourselves off the hook. It is difficult for any of us to see ourselves the way God sees us, or even the way others see us. Denial is not God's way of escape.

Some people take flight from reality by compulsive behavior. They cram their lives with activity—often needless activity—simply because they cannot live with themselves. They compulsively overeat, overspend, or overschedule. To deaden the pain of loneliness and emotional emptiness, many resort to illicit sexual relationships and other destructive friendships.

Drugs and alcohol are other popular escape routes. Almost daily the media tells us about someone who died of an overdose of drugs.

What is forgotten are the tens of thousands of addicts who die slowly, bit by bit, day by day.

With ten million alcoholics among us, we have had many examples of mindless escapism. Far from drowning problems, alcohol actually irrigates them, causing them to grow much stronger. Payday cannot be endlessly postponed.

These escape routes only perpetuate the power of the past, rather than defeat it.

What Is God's Way of Escape?

Biblical escape routes take many forms, but they always have these characteristics. First, there is honesty. The acting must end.

The lies that have covered the sin must be exposed. God will deal with us only on the basis of truth, not evasion. Honesty is also necessary for those who have been the victim of other people's sins. No one can close the door to his past without taking a look at it and "making peace" with all that is there.

Second, there is humility. To be willing to do anything that God requires—even sharing our past with some of our friends who can pray for us in our need—is necessary. There are times when we cannot put our past behind us alone; we need the assistance of others. Yes, the divine surgeon wants to lance our wounds so the poison can be released. Doctors tell us that in physical surgery a large area has to be cut out so that it can heal as a clean wound. Time is needed; to scrape the scab only delays the healing process. Just so, God heals our spiritual wounds, giving us the grace to forgive and be forgiven. He is a healing God.

Some people have been able to put a painful past behind them rapidly, perhaps at the moment of conversion. Others have needed more time but have not had to recall the details of all the hurt they experienced. Then there are those who will never be at peace until they have carefully looked at their past and dealt with all the hurts, one at a time. For some, just coping more effectively is progress.

So what is the way of escape? It is through matching the power of God with the deepest level of human need. *It is learning that God is with us even if the hurts will not go away.*

In the presence of God and His grace there is hope for a new beginning. Someone has said that when God closes a door, He opens a window. And when He gives us a trial, He gives us the shoulders to bear it.

I don't want to proclaim a God who is only capable of delivering people from small sins or helping those who come from stable families. God is able to bring even the most hopeless up from the miry clay, set their feet upon a rock, and help them learn to walk. And even if the wounds of the past never heal, these people can live productive lives, knowing that present suffering cannot be compared with the glory that awaits them.

THE SEARCH FOR A NEW BEGINNING

Let's sketch the big picture, get a glimpse of our predicament, and look at the first step needed to put the past behind us.

When the naturalist Thoreau was close to death, he was visited by a pious aunt, who asked, "Henry, have you made your peace with God?"

"I didn't know we had quarreled," he replied.

Thoreau was as far from the truth as one could travel. All of us have had our quarrel with God. Our problem is that we don't want to admit we've quarreled and that, in the end, He is always the winner.

For starters, we are born into this world under the condemnation of sin. Unfair? Think of it this way: If you were born into a family that was greatly in debt, those debts would be passed on to you even though you had not personally incurred them. When Adam sinned, we all sinned with him—we participated in his decision in the sense that he, as the father of the human race, represented all of us.

That is only the beginning of our problem. As we grow older, we begin to behave like the sinners we are. The idea that evil is something we do because of the bad examples around us, and not because of the fundamental flaw within us, is naive and contrary to experience.

As we grow into adulthood, behavior patterns become entrenched; and without inner restraints, we tend to follow our desires wherever they lead. This begins a cycle of behavior we simultaneously love and hate.

Most people think the solution to their predicament rests with themselves. They may swear off their old habits, or even join a self-help group, and notice some dramatic improvements. Though these changes are good, they can ultimately be harmful if they become a substitute for God's answer to their dilemma. The good has become the enemy of the best.

Self-improvement cannot rectify our quarrel with God. Nor can it take away the guilt that accompanies sinful behavior. It can only redirect it. Thus, guilt reappears under different labels. Too often it is pushed into the subconscious.

What is God's answer to our sinfulness? To ask the question differently, how can a sinner become just before God? To put it briefly, Christ's death on the cross was a sacrifice for sin. This means God is able to actually credit us with the righteousness of Christ.

"For our sake he made him to be sin who knew no sin, so that in him we might become the righteousness of God" (2 Cor. 5:21). God is not waiting to clobber wayward sinners who dare to stagger into His presence. We've all heard of earthly fathers who can hardly wait to whip their children into line; but our heavenly Father invites sinners to dinner, binds up their wounds, and pours grace into their souls.

Like the father of the prodigal, our Father in heaven calls for the best robe (a symbol of honor), the shoes (a symbol of acceptance), and the fatted calf (a symbol of fellowship). He waits for sinners not with a club but with a cup of mercy and grace.

The good news is that this act of God clears our record once for all. He declares us as righteous as Christ. "Truly, truly, I say to you, whoever hears my word and believes him who sent me has eternal life. He does not come into judgment, but has passed from death to life" (John 5:24).

This gift of righteousness is not given to everyone but is limited to those who admit their own helplessness and transfer all of their trust to Christ alone. God justifies the ungodly when they give up trusting themselves and believe in His Son.

Is that the end of the story? If God accepts us on the basis of Christ's merit, do we ever have to confess our sins again? And does this mean we can sin as much as we please? What about those tattoos still branded onto our souls? Is there really hope for a new beginning?

These and other questions will be answered in the chapters that follow.

Read on.

ACTION STEP

Spend one unhurried hour singing hymns of praise to God and reviewing the promises of Scripture. Remember that faith in God's goodness toward you is essential in order to cope with your painful past.

Chapter 2

Ending the Denial Game

At a county fair, I walked into a house of mirrors. Because of the curvature of the glass, one mirror made me look tall; another made me look fat; and another, lopsided. I went from being a giant to being as small as a child. I could not predict how I would look from one room to the next. There were as many different representations of me as there were mirrors on the walls.

We all want a mirror that makes us look good. In fact, if the mirrors around us don't make us look good, we will construct one that does. Instinctively, we want to hide our true selves and project an image that makes us appear to be appealing, worthy, and loved. And the way we hope to see ourselves is the way we hope others see us. We can see this deception clearly in others, but it exists in us, too.

This mental sleight of hand is known as denial, a fundamental unwillingness to let others see our dark side. Denial causes us to set up defenses so that we won't have to face reality. We try to hide who we really are for the sake of reputation and self-preservation. All information that comes to us about ourselves is filtered, so that only what we like passes through the grid of our psyches.

Denial is not a problem that belongs only to the families of alcoholics, or to abusers or criminals. We've all projected an image that is not true; we have encouraged people to think better of us than we deserve. And sometimes our deception has created a chasm between who we really are and whom others perceive us to be. We often call this discrepancy our "blind spot."

As you read this chapter, resist the temptation to apply it to people you know rather than to yourself. Admitting who we are is the first step to becoming who we should be.

TWO KINDS OF DENIAL

Swiss theologian Karl Barth has rightly pointed out that we are all incorrigible liars. Because we live under the dominion of sin, we lie both to God and to ourselves. We will fight against any encroachment of light that uncovers the hidden closets of the soul.

Conscious denial means that we are quite aware of the gap that exists between our public image and our private lifestyle. The man who meticulously hides his pornography is very conscious of the discrepancy between who he really is and how he wants to be perceived. The woman who is stealing funds from her company has gone to such great lengths to cover her misdeeds that she probably has attracted some unwanted attention in the office. In other matters she is scrupulously honest so that she can congratulate herself for being a "good person" after all.

Those who live with a spouse who is in obvious denial know how protective such a person can be. The man who drinks alone every night, convincing himself that he is not an alcoholic, will fight against the reality check his family seeks to give him. Addicts of all sorts are masters of denial and cannot be helped until their illusory bubble breaks.

Someone has said that if we were made of glass, so that whatever was within us could be seen, we would all want to live alone on desert islands! Of course, some have more to hide than others; they find it necessary to play manipulative games to keep themselves hidden. The child molester, drug addict, and adulterer become skilled in the denial game for survival purposes. Most of them know the truth—but also know the tricks for keeping it hidden.

Think of the emotional schizophrenia caused by a secret adulterous relationship. When a man's whole life is a charade and keeping a secret becomes his obsession, every brush with reality must be held in check. His heart is hardened to deaden the pain, and his mind is on full alert, rationalizing, excusing, and denying.

Conscious denial can lead to unconscious denial. When we set out to deceive others, we often end up deceiving ourselves. We've all known people who have actually come to believe their own falsehoods. Although some might argue that it is impossible for us to believe what we know to be false, more than a few people have actually accomplished this feat. A Christian man who ran off with another man's wife said that they had prayed about it and were convinced that their relationship was God's will. Can anyone doubt that he believed the deceptions of his own heart?

Self-deception is a defense mechanism, a protective maneuver that shields a person from the pain of reality. Often there are hidden motives of the heart that are not consciously recognized; these interpret reality in such a way that it comes out to the person's liking. Remember, by nature we are in conflict with ourselves, actively fighting against the truth we intuitively know.

Pascal, a French philosopher, said that we as humans plunge heedlessly toward the abyss, deliberately shielding our eyes from what we know is there. Though we have a suspicion that we know what is wrong, we take great pains to cover our faults from others and even from ourselves. Perhaps the preacher had a great deal of wisdom when he was told by one of his parishioners, "I know something is wrong in my life, but I don't know what it is." The parson's advice: "Just get on your knees and guess at it!"

Augustine said that before his conversion his "impiety divided me against myself."[5] The prophet Jeremiah believed that we were incapable of understanding the deceit that lurks within our own hearts. "The heart is deceitful above all things, and desperately sick; who can understand it? 'I the LORD search the heart and test the mind, to give every man according to his ways, according to the fruit of his deeds'" (Jer. 17:9–10). Only God can understand the complete depths of our motives, desires, and unconscious longings.

Paul agreed that self-deception is possible: "For if anyone thinks he is something, when he is nothing, he deceives himself" (Gal. 6:3). Evidently, there are people who actually think they are something, blissfully unaware that they are "nothing." Since they deny who they actually are, they are free to live in an imaginary world of their own making—a world in which they are heroes and others the villains. James says that if people look into God's mirror and then walk away forgetting what they saw, they are only hearers of the word, not doers, and deceive themselves (James 1:22).

Surely the unconverted are self-deceived. Paul wrote that they "by their unrighteousness suppress the truth" (Rom. 1:18). We've all tried to use our thumb to stop the water pressure as it flows through the end of a garden hose. Just so, the unrighteous fight against what they know is true. Repression makes it possible for them to live in a world of their own making rather than face the reality of who they really are before God. Interestingly, Peter writes that those who deny that God is the creator are "willingly . . . ignorant" (2 Peter 3:5 KJV).

Put simply, the human mind is able to rationalize anything that the human heart wants to do. The mind is capable of every form of lying, posturing, hedging, and reinterpreting the facts in order to maintain a carefully crafted reputation. Eventually these lies can be believed, and illusion can be perceived as the truth. Such deceptions die hard.

The fact is that we simply don't know as much about ourselves as we think; most of all, we are quite unaware of our potential for evil.

REASONS FOR DENIAL

Denial Enables Us to Avoid Blame

When Adam and Eve sinned in the garden, they covered themselves with leaves and put the best possible spin on their behavior. When Adam was asked point-blank by God whether he had eaten of the forbidden tree, he pointed to his wife: "The woman whom thou gavest to be with me, she gave me of the tree, and I did eat" (Gen. 3:12 KJV). Adam blamed his wife, even though there wasn't a chance that he had married the wrong one!

Humans are ingenious in projecting blame. We can see virtually all of our conflicts as the fault of our spouses, our children, our employers, the government. We turn our eyes away from the flat mirror to find one that has the right curvature to embellish our image. We carefully construct our own version of how things are. Intuitively, we know that a bent person can look straight if the truth is bent instead. Keeping others from seeing ourselves for what we are is our lifelong challenge.

Denial Helps Us Avoid Pain

Physical pain, no matter how excruciating, is much more welcome than the emotional pain of facing what we have done or what has been done to us. For a child abuser, breaking a leg is not nearly as painful as the torment of exposure. And for the victim, the pain (or fear) of admitting what a parent has done is so terrifying that children might block it out of their minds or create the illusory world we referred to earlier.

Denial becomes a cocoon, providing refuge from the dreadful storm abuser and victim alike would encounter if their carefully constructed walls were to collapse. Unfortunately, this cocoon offers only limited and temporary protection. As we shall see, we can only be healed by coming out, by breaking the shell.

Sometimes grief, even pain over the death of a friend, is also denied for fear that open sorrow will be interpreted as weakness or an unspiritual response to the loss. If you are told, for example, that good Christians do not have to go through the stages of grief, you will be tempted to keep your real feelings suppressed.

Denial Is a Defense Maneuver to Avoid Shame

Sexual sins of various kinds are especially prone to generate guilt and personal disgrace. The shame of adultery, homosexuality, or cross-dressing, for example, can be powerful. A woman who happened to return home unexpectedly one afternoon discovered her husband prancing around the living room in women's clothes, a sexually stimulating experience for him. The humiliation of having to admit to this long-standing practice was so devastating that he stopped attending church and eventually had to leave the area. Shame is one of the most powerful of all human emotions and will spawn all forms of denial and rationalization.

Of course, the perpetrator of abuse lives in denial. Only God knows the mental energy he uses to keep his behavior secret. Christ said, "For everyone who does wicked things hates the light and does not come to the light, lest his works should be exposed" (John 3:20). Like vermin, the guilty run when the rock is overturned. Such prefer darkness to sunshine, a cave rather than a hilltop.

Think of what it means to grow up in a home where you are ashamed of your parents, or your parents shame you. You cannot invite classmates to your home; you are too embarrassed to let anyone know what really happens behind closed doors. Children are driven to secrecy and the fear that they are abnormal, weird, and unlovable. Everyone in the home has to play the denial game.

Some mistreated children will even develop alternate personalities to cope with the pain of reality. Their desire to believe the best about their parents is so strong that they would rather blame themselves for the abuse than blame their parents. An imaginary world is created where everything turns out just right.

This world is purposely disconnected from reality. Eventually it takes on a life of its own; fantasy is substituted for reality.

CHARACTERISTICS OF DENIAL

What are the characteristics of those who live in denial?

An Inability to Express Feelings

First, there is emotional numbness. Some cannot cry or express emotions, whether anger or grief. To reveal their feelings would put an end to the game that is played day after day. If the mask is to be worn, the emotions must be turned off like a spigot.

One woman explained that as a child she was taught to ignore her feelings. She was shamed whenever she expressed anger, sadness, joy, or hope. She felt she was the cause of her father's alcoholism and irrational anger. She grew up trying to be a good little girl so that her father wouldn't have to drink.

In such a family, feelings don't count; this little girl used all of her energy to hide her emotions to maintain some kind of order in her chaotic home. "The code of silence was so strong that it never entered my mind to explain my problem to the teachers. When I left the house in the morning, I would act as if I were the happiest child in the world. I was not only lying to the world but to myself." The power of denial.

She continued, "We all learned to lie—we lied to Daddy's boss;

31

we lied to our friends. On the one hand, we were told not to lie; on the other hand, we were not allowed to tell the truth. When I came of age, my marriage was doomed from the start. I told my parents on a Wednesday that I was pregnant and was married quickly on a Friday so that no one would know the truth. It was the saddest day of my life. My father was drunk at the wedding . . . I felt suicidal."

Thankfully, the man she married was not an alcoholic, but a rather decent husband. But this woman felt she had to create one crisis after another to maintain the dysfunctional relationships she had known. She became supercritical of her husband, and to find fulfillment, had an affair with another man whom she later married. But she kept her previous lifestyle from him, carefully crafting a story he believed for two years. When the truth came to light, her marriage felt the tremors of another emotional earthquake.

Those who are forced to turn off their feelings as children often live as adults on "cruise control." They simply cannot find it within themselves to face the reality of their pain. Their emotions are numb; the tears seldom come. Though the problems in their home would be obvious to any healthy person, the members of the dysfunctional family refuse to see the aberrations. The game must be played.

Superficial Relationships

A second consequence of denial is superficial friendships. Understandably so, for a deep friendship is based on the assumption that I am free to share my dreams, my hopes, my fears. But if the unwritten rules in the home do not allow for honest expression, all communication must be limited to the trivia of day-to-day living. Questions are used only to clarify the obvious, and talk is reduced to the minimum phrases necessary among those who exist in the same house.

Meaningful communication is also blocked by selective listening. A child may try to get his father to hear his point of view, feel his grief, and understand his shame. But the father will not listen.

In many instances he will break into the conversation mid-sentence. Then he will clarify his own viewpoint, such as it is, leaving no room for discussion. His personal philosophy is "Let's compromise and do it my way!"

Communication is kept to a minimum because someone might shoot an arrow and pierce the carefully crafted cocoon. Remember, nothing personal can be revealed; no faults on the father's part can be exposed. The mirror must always reflect what he wants others to see.

Imagine what denial does to a marriage. Many a man, married for years, has never paused to try to understand life from his wife's point of view. Her hopes, dreams, fears, and goals have never been revealed. Though the two of them share the same house and even the same bedroom, they live in different emotional worlds. The man protects himself from his wife; she protects herself from her husband. Neither is willing to develop a deep friendship. Reality is always held at arm's length.

Lack of Trust

Not surprisingly, another symptom is lack of trust. When a person has been hurt or has hurt someone else, he or she assumes that the world is a cruel place where no one is to be trusted. Those who live in denial find it difficult to give and receive love. This is understandable, for love is a giving of oneself. Denial enables a person to withhold his true self from others.

This lack of trust can extend to everyone we know. If those who are closest to us have forced us to play an elaborate game, we certainly cannot trust those who are a part of an even wider circle. If a father, who should protect his children, abuses them, how can they trust a teacher at school or even friends at church, or a marriage partner?

Somewhere I read a story about two intoxicated men who left a bar to walk home. One of them did not realize that someone had smeared some strong-smelling cheese under his nose. As he walked into the clear night air he muttered, "The whole world stinks!"

As fallen creatures we soon learn that one way to decrease our own pain is to maximize the faults of other people and minimize our own. When our faults are revealed, we will fight by angrily pointing to those who have done something worse, often attacking the very person who has probed beneath our veneer. We measure ourselves by a carefully selected group and conclude that we couldn't be that bad, really. Once again, we choose a mirror that makes someone else look bent but makes us look just about right. When confronted with reality, we insist that there is some reason, some extenuating circumstance, some event that will put everything in its "true" light. Like David when Nathan used the story of the sheep to confront him for adultery, we see other people's sins with amazing clarity but are blind to our own. David told the prophet that the man who stole a sheep should pay fourfold! He refused to acknowledge that he had not only stolen a wife but had killed her husband. When we live in denial, the life of a lamb seems more important than the life of a human being.

Perfectionism

Codependents—that is, persons who have grown up in dysfunctional homes—will often become perfectionists, trying to make up for the deficiencies of their own families. They can be critical, demanding, and controlling. Sometimes, they persevere in the illusion that they are living in an ordered world. To compensate for the chaos of their youth, they seek to make sure that every detail of their lives is now well-ordered. Though it does not change the basic root problem, perfectionism will let a person live with the delusion that everything is really quite fine after all. This carefully constructed image, no matter how deceitful, continues to be meticulously maintained.

Dishonesty forces us to suppress our conscience, which sits in judgment of our thoughts and actions. If our guilt is not cleansed by God, we will have to live with it, resolving the tension as best we can. Even our clearest days will be marred by emotional clouds that will not go away. When one lie leads to another, the conscience must be silenced. As we have learned, this is done through elaborate rationalizations (projecting guilt on others) or by comparison (finding someone worse than oneself). In such an emotional state, we also must maintain our distance from God. The Bible is not read, prayer is never serious, and confession is not deep. Superficiality in relationships with others spills over into one's relationship with God. We all, I think, can identify with Hamlet:

> *My words fly up, my thoughts remain below.*
> *Words without thoughts never to heaven go.*
> (3.3.97)

Why is sin so deceitful? "But exhort one another every day, as long as it is called 'today,' that none of you may be hardened by the deceitfulness of sin" (Heb. 3:13). Sin never comes to us in its true light. A person who is deceived does not know it! He actually believes the mirror he has chosen is correct, no matter how skewed it is in the light of God's revealed Word. When you believe a lie, it becomes the truth for you.

Some people who live in denial are quite honest when they say that they don't see their faults. "I don't lose my temper; I just want to be the leader of our home." Or "I have my drinking, but I deserve a bit of pleasure, considering the stress that I am under." Or "I'm not manipulative; I just like to see things done right." Such a person has a foolproof defense system. He thinks he really is okay.

Manipulation

Finally, those who are in denial often resort to manipulation. The addict uses his power to impose guilt on his family so that they

35

will play the game according to his rules. The guilt and shame he rightfully feels are used as weapons against others. The denial game becomes the blame game.

Of course, there are many levels of denial and many different ways that it makes its appearance; but the longer we refuse to see the truth, the harder our hearts become.

Thankfully, there is a better way.

The Fear and Joy of Exposure

Robert Fulghum, in *All I Really Need to Know I Learned in Kindergarten,* tells how in October when he was a child, he and his friends would play hide-and-seek under the leaves. There was always one kid who hid so well nobody could find him. Eventually, the others gave up on him. When he finally showed up, they would explain to him that there is hiding and there is finding, and he was not to hide in such a way that he could not be found.

Fulghum continues:

> As I write this, the neighborhood game goes on, and there is a kid under a pile of leaves in the yard just under my window. He has been there a long time now, and everybody else is found and they are about to give up on him over at the base. I considered going out to the base and telling them where he is hiding. And I thought about setting the leaves on fire to drive him out. Finally, I just yelled, "GET FOUND, KID!" out the window. And scared him so bad he probably . . . started crying and ran home to tell his mother. It's real hard to know how to be helpful sometimes.[6]

We play hide-and-seek grown-up style. We want to hide so well we will never be found, even to our detriment. We have all hidden under stacks of leaves arranged so skillfully that no one can see us. At first it is fun, but later it is a private hell. Eventually, no matter how long we have been hiding, no matter why we are hiding, we want to be found. In fact, we cannot be helped unless we are found!

How do we end the denial game?

"Only God knows who I really am, and may He graciously preserve me from finding out," the Enlightenment scholar Goethe is quoted as saying. Yes, it is true that God knows who we are, but it is also true that only when He shows us ourselves is there hope and forgiveness. If Goethe had but allowed God to show him who he was, he might have found what he so desperately needed.

We Must Admit That We've Already Been Found Out!

David came to terms with who he was when he grasped the fact that God knew him completely, "Lord, You have searched me and known me. You know when I sit down and when I get up; You understand my thought from far away. You scrutinize my path and my lying down, and are acquainted with all my ways" (Ps. 139:1–3 NASB).

David was aware that God knew him exhaustively. The Almighty knew the number of times he sat down or stood up; He knew every word that David had ever spoken; and, more ominously, knew every one of his thoughts before they even arose in his mind! In the presence of God there are no secrets, no buried motives, no bent mirrors. We are who we are, without excuses or carefully crafted explanations.

God knows us continually. "Where shall I go from your Spirit? Or where shall I flee from your presence? If I ascend to heaven, you are there! If I make my bed in Sheol, you are there!" (Ps. 139:7–8). If we think we can run from God, we should remember that He exists in the remotest part of the universe. He travels where light has not yet penetrated; He exists beyond the edges of the universe.

David, despairing of trying to run from God, contemplates hiding from Him in the dark. But "even the darkness is not dark to you; the night is bright as the day, for darkness is as light with you" (v. 12).

Criminals do their work in the cover of darkness, but in God's sight they are acting at high noon. For God there are no hidden places. We can never talk about God behind His back; we can never do something in the dark that is kept from the watchful eye of the Almighty. God knows the facts, all of them. "All things are open and laid bare to the eyes of Him to whom we must answer" (Heb. 4:13 NASB).

In fact, God knew David eternally. "Your eyes saw my unformed substance; in your book were written, every one of them, the days that were formed for me, when as yet there was none of them" (Ps. 139:16). God knew him when he was fashioned in his mother's womb. David had no secrets.

Imagine a series of books that contained every word you ever uttered. It has been estimated that most people speak enough words in their lifetime to fill a good-sized library. (Obviously, we've met some people whose library is much greater than it should be!) Add to this the books that contain every action you ever did, from your earliest cries to your present schedule. Every step you took, every nod of the head and blink of the eyes. That in itself would add many shelves to your personal library. Finally, add the books that contain every thought you have ever had. These books would be more numerous than all the others combined. *All this about you!*

But we are not finished yet. Suppose this library contained all the information that would have been true of you if you had been reared in a different family, under different circumstances, and in a different era. Such information would have to be included because God knows what we would have done or said under different circumstances. Remember, His knowledge includes not only that which is actual but also that which would be possible under other conditions.

All this knowledge exists in God's mind. Not one single bit of information has escaped His attention. All the thoughts we are glad no one has ever seen are present to God. He knows the coverups, the lies, the manipulation, the playacting. He has found us.

Adam and Eve thought that if they covered themselves with leaves and hid behind a tree, God might come seeking but would not find. But God saw through the trees and the fig leaves. Even while hiding beneath a tree, they were already found.

Perhaps now we better understand why hell is just. We often think that only the likes of a Stalin or Hitler should be so judged. But when God judges the unconverted, all their defenses will be demolished. They will see themselves as God sees them, which, incidentally, is a definition of reality. Then hell will appear both just and appropriate.

Though God's intimate knowledge is fearsome, it is also comforting. Those of you who have been abused, those of you who have gone through the shame of living with a parent who falsely accused you, be encouraged by the fact that God knows the whole story. Though some might not believe you, God is not seduced by the smooth talk of the wicked. He knows what others are not willing to admit. He was watching everything, and it is all recorded.

We Must Invite God to Search Us

What is our response to this knowledge? David prayed, "Search me, O God, and know my heart! Try me and know my thoughts! And see if there be any grievous way in me, and lead me in the way everlasting!" (Ps. 139:23–24).

Why does David now ask God to search him when he has already affirmed that God knows him entirely? David is saying, "God, I know that You know everything there is to know about me; now show me what You see!"

Finally, David was willing to see himself in God's mirror. He would see a clearer image without alibis, without shifting blame, without a carefully crafted spin on the details. Just him, alone, in the presence of an all-knowing God.

God lets us see at least a bit of what He sees. We will never see ourselves exactly as He sees us, but we will see enough of reality to be brought to repentance. Perhaps we will also see ourselves the way others see us. We will see sins and attitudes we did not know existed. Our self-perception, which was out of kilter, will, at least to some extent, be revealed. Other people can help us if we have the humility to accept their critique; but in the end, only God can help us see the whole horrid mess.

Pascal said, "Not only do we know God through Jesus Christ; we can only know ourselves through Jesus Christ." The knowledge of ourselves is only possible through our knowledge of God. He is the standard by which we can come to know who we really are. He's the only one with a straight mirror.

We Must Share Our Secrets with One Other Human Being Whom We Trust

We all need at least one person who will love us even if we have to confess that which is truly evil. Getting the secret out in the open is necessary to bring healing. A policeman told me that even criminals want to be discovered. They are weary of bearing the heavy burden of deception. Deep within, they want to be exposed, pay for their sin, and ease their own consciences.

Deception cannot end as long as we do not acknowledge the truth of the past. Abusers must admit to the truth; so must alcoholics, adulterers, and those who have hurt others by their insensitivity and anger. We must renounce "disgraceful, underhanded ways. We refuse to practice cunning or to tamper with God's word, but by the open statement of the truth we would commend ourselves to everyone's conscience in the sight of God" (2 Cor. 4:2).

Robert Munger, in his booklet *My Heart: Christ's Home,* describes how we must invite Christ into the different rooms of our hearts: the den with its TV set, the kitchen with its food, and the living room with its reading material. But, Munger says, we often refuse to invite Christ into a closet we have determined to keep closed.

With God we can walk through the secret closets of our lives, opening them one by one. And even those closets that we fear to open, those cubbyholes we have carefully bolted shut, are not too much for us and God. To open those doors alone is fearful, but God will not only show us where the closets are but will help pry open the door.

And so I shout to you, "Get found!"

ACTION STEP

Wait quietly before God for one hour, inviting the Holy Spirit to search your heart, revealing those issues that need to be faced in your life. Write on a sheet of paper the matters that you know you must resolve in the presence of God.

Pray David's prayer, "Search me, O God, and know my heart! Try me and know my thoughts! And see if there be any grievous way in me, and lead me in the way everlasting!" (Ps. 139:23–24).

Chapter 3

Pardon for the Unpardonable

The voice of conscience has driven many a person to an early grave. It may begin as a whisper but eventually can blare like a megaphone, nudging its victim over the brink. For some, it leads to an undefined sense of depression; for others it is a call to wanton pleasure. No pleading or logic can silence the voice that tells us we are unclean, unworthy, and doomed to the hopelessness we know we deserve.

"I see babies everywhere, and they seem to look at me like they know what I did was wrong. I see little boys with their parents, and it hurts so much. I just want to crawl in a hole and die." This is the lament of a man who encouraged his girlfriend to get an abortion since he "cared about 'what other people thought.'" Now he realizes that he killed his son. He "has trouble repenting because he doesn't know who to talk to." Years later, he keeps "looking over his shoulder," expecting God's wrath.[7]

We've already learned that we cannot resolve our guilt by resorting to denial, pretending that we are good when in fact we know otherwise. We must face who we are in the presence of the only one who can clean us up and bring peace to our troubled hearts. The greater our honesty, the greater our joy.

The purpose of this chapter is to show why any sin, no matter how evil, can be forgiven by God. This is an invitation to accept God's promise that even criminals can take to heart; there is no sin, whether public or hidden, that God cannot forgive.

Even those who have had the good fortune of being raised in relatively stable families know the power of guilt. Many children know they have not lived up to their parents' expectations. Their mothers and fathers continually remind them (often with severe discipline) that they have failed. Since a child's first understanding of who he is comes from his parents, this lack of acceptance is a tremendous blow to his self-esteem.

Guilt is amplified in the lives of children who are abused; they wrongly assume they are simply getting what they deserve. They believe they are as bad as their parents make them out to be. *If Mom and Dad think I am that evil, I must be!* the child reasons.

Understandably, the burden becomes overwhelming. Some children feel guilty for just being alive, and they bring those unresolved emotions into their adult lives. This is false guilt, of course, but it can be just as destructive as real guilt.

Some of us would say that our guilt began when our schoolteachers expressed disapproval of our performance. We knew that our value depended on our report card. We felt insecurity and a feeling of worthlessness. We feared we would be the last in our class, the one on the lowest rung of the acceptance ladder.

Of course, we have also disappointed ourselves, and this makes forgiveness difficult. We make foolish decisions, fail, and commit one sin after another. We know we have betrayed our basic values and think we are unworthy hypocrites. We have the track record to prove it. More guilt.

Finally, the greatest condemnation resting on our souls is the constant realization that we have disappointed *God.* Try as we might, we intuitively know He demands even more. Our misery is compounded by our awareness that He knows our whole story. God knows the young woman killed her infant daughter in an abortion clinic; God knows the young man had a series of homosexual trysts that led other young men into a similar lifestyle. God knows, and the perpetrators know that God knows! Since the possibility of our ever appeasing a wrathful God is the most enduring of all illusions, we are doomed to keep trying, only to keep failing.

Many people assume they will be banished from the presence of the Lord without a lot of fanfare. Like Cain, they believe their burdens are heavier than they can bear. They would agree, with David, that their sin is "ever before" them (Ps. 51:3).

CONTINUING CONSEQUENCES OF GUILT

What does guilt do to us? William Justice describes the effects of a disquieted conscience, which he calls "the cycle of the damned." Listen to his description:

For every failure to live up to some "ought," there is the tendency to punish oneself in such a manner as to produce another failure! And every failure produces the response, I ought not to have failed! I stand convicted of having violated an "ought" that in turn produces the need for further punishment which results in further failure.

Having failed, I punish myself in such a manner as to produce a further sense of failure. A cycle is completed only to begin again. I have failed to live up to some "ought" for which I feel guilty. Convicted of guilt, I feel the need to pay. To pay, I choose a method that will leave me with a sense of having failed. On and on rolls the cycle downward. It may be compared to a snowball rolling down a hill, adding to its own momentum with each revolution . . . this cycle goes round and round, down and down and down, and has the potential of going on and on eternally. That is at least one aspect of hell![8]

Justice tells of a young man who was hospitalized for heroin addiction. When a chaplain asked him why he was knowingly blowing his mind on drugs, he replied that anyone ought to know the answer to that question. "I feel so bad about some of the things I've done, I want to die. I don't have the guts to pick up a gun and blow my brains out, so I just do it the slow way by drugs. I feel like I ought'a have to pay for what all I've done wrong. I think most of us who are using this stuff feel the same way."[9]

This, observed Justice, is death on the installment plan. Some pay through addiction; others pay through crime. The criminal often is doing more than simply "earning a living" by breaking the law. He is living dangerously so as to be punished. Getting caught doesn't change him; he feels unworthy of living a better life. As soon as he can, he will repeat his cycle of destructive behavior. Going unpunished may be even worse for him than being caught. Lady Macbeth, an accomplice in the death of Duncan the king, thought her bloodstained hands could be washed clean easily. "A little water clears us of this deed," she assured her husband.

But her husband had already told the truth:

Will all great Neptune's ocean wash this blood
 Clean from my hand?
No, this my hand will rather
 The multitudinous seas incarnadine,
Making the green one red.
  (2.2.60–67)

Though Lady Macbeth began by thinking her guilt could be erased easily, she finally gave in to the loud protestations of a defiled conscience and cried, "Here's the smell of the blood still: all the per-fumes of Arabia will not sweeten this little hand" (5.1.54–55). When the mental torture became unbearable, she did what thirty thousand Americans do every year—she committed suicide. There is a feeling deep within us that sin can be forgiven only if blood is shed. Of course, this is exactly what the Bible teaches: "Without the shedding of blood there is no forgiveness of sins" (Heb. 9:22). But some people pervert this teaching by shedding their own blood in a desperate but futile attempt to pay what their conscience tells them they owe.

THE UNPARDONABLE SIN

Immorality, child abuse, rape, and murder—these sins and others like them have driven many into the inner chambers of a personal hell. They exist in the darkness of remorse, self-hatred, and guilt. Their private torture drives them to conclude that their sin is unpardonable.

A man who unintentionally passed a sexually transmitted disease to his wife cursed himself and God for his past sins. "I don't want God's forgiveness even if He would give it to me," he complained angrily, "because no matter what happens I deserve to burn in hell." Unable to forgive himself, he saw no benefit to God's forgiveness. He thought his sin was unpardonable.

Read this letter I received from another tortured young man:

Last Saturday night I was tempted to commit the unpardon-able sin. Ever since I found out about this sin four years ago, I was worried about committing it. Well, last Saturday night it happened: I became angry and I started cursing God and calling the Holy Spirit blasphemous and insulting names.

Then I asked for forgiveness, but nothing seemed to go right, so I began to get even angrier, and I cursed. Do you think I got God so angry that He left me?

I know I should give up a friendship with a man who is immersed in pornography—but I have not done it.

I didn't sleep all night because I was so upset and so worried that I had committed this sin. Do you think Satan is making me real gloomy so that I think I have committed this sin?

Christ did speak of an unpardonable sin, but what did He mean? What is it?

The Pharisees had seen the miracles of Christ and attributed them to Satan. Christ pointed out that their conclusion was illogical. Satan would never think of casting out his own accomplices (demons). Satan does not cast out Satan. Only a person who is stronger than Satan can cast him out.

Christ then adds:

Therefore I tell you, every sin and blasphemy will be forgiven people, but the blasphemy against the Spirit will not be forgiven. And whoever speaks a word against the Son of Man will be forgiven, but whoever speaks against the Holy Spirit will not be forgiven, either in this age or in the age to come. (Matt. 12:31–32)

The unpardonable sin was committed when the spiritual rulers stood between Christ and the common people, who were willing to accept Christ's miracles as legitimate. In the context of the New Testament, this sin was that of an unbelieving nation that had lost its spiritual sensitivity and determinedly rejected God's Messiah. Spiritual blindness rested upon that generation of Israelites (with the exception of the believers), and they were excluded from God's grace and loving-kindness in Christ.

Why was forgiveness impossible?

It is necessary to *believe* in order to be forgiven! The Pharisees who rejected Christ's credentials were excluding themselves from the kingdom of heaven by their unbelief. In trying to extinguish the light, they were becoming so hard-hearted they did not desire forgiveness.

Note well that the unpardonable sin was committed only by unbelievers, that is, those who did not receive Christ for salvation. They had nurtured a hard heart; thus they had to accept the consequences of their decision.

This sin cannot be committed in the same sense today because (1) Christ is not on the earth performing miracles to convince us that He is the Messiah, and (2) this sin was the Jews' national rejection of Christ. Today faith healers claim to do miracles, though many of us have doubts about the validity of these claims. Such doubt is not a sin, but simply the honest opinion of those who try to evaluate such phenomena.

Some people today, however, do commit *an* unpardonable sin through their persistent rejection of Christ. They neither seek repentance, nor desire it. They simply choose to crowd Christ out of their lives, and, like the Pharisees, live with the result. These are the reprobates, the unconverted who no longer sense the need for God's forgiveness. They never were saved and don't desire to be.

Be assured that if you are concerned about having committed the unpardonable sin, you have not done so! Your sensitivity proves that God is working in your heart. Those who commit an unpardonable sin have no concern whatever about their relationship with Him. Obviously, pardon is available only for those who want it.

The man who wrote the above letter must first settle the question of whether he is a Christian. If he is, his next step is to repent of all sin that the Holy Spirit brings to his attention. If necessary, he also should receive counsel from mature believers, who can bring him to the assurance of forgiveness. Thankfully, his sin is not unpardonable.

If you, dear reader, believe your sin is unpardonable, or if you know someone who believes he has crossed the line that leads to the abyss of unrelenting regret and a tortured conscience, you must know that there is hope. Night settles on the soul, but the Son can rise.

Pardon is available and you can receive it. To help you be assured that you are forgiven, let me explain the concepts of forgiveness and grace in the New Testament. *There is more grace in God's heart than there is sin in your past.*

THE PATH TO PARDON

Ponder these words:

> And you, who were dead in your trespasses and the uncircumcision of your flesh, God made alive together with him, having forgiven us all our trespasses, by canceling the record of debt that stood against us with its legal demands. This he set aside, nailing it to the cross. (Col. 2:13–14)

Paul is referring to an ancient custom where the paid debts of an individual were listed on a piece of parchment with "Paid in Full" written on it. Then it was nailed on a public billboard so all could see that the debts were paid.

When Christ died on the cross, He took all the debts we as lawbreakers owed God, and *He paid them.* God the Father received that payment and was fully satisfied with it. Figuratively speaking, the bill that was paid was nailed to the cross for all to see.

Incredibly, as Christians we do not owe God any righteousness—Jesus met our obligations for us. His words on the cross, "It is finished!" (John 19:30), are but one word in Greek, and it means "Paid in full!" Thus, we can stand before God fully accepted; we have the same standing before Him as Christ. Yes, even sins of blasphemy can be forgiven.

Here is the starting point for a clear conscience. Remember that Christ's death was payment for all we have done, *past, present,* and *future.* Since He died two thousand years before we were born, His sacrifice included sins that we have not yet committed. God anticipated our sins—and these in their entirety were laid on Christ. If you are a Christian, there is no sin you will ever commit that has not *already* been paid for.

A popular misconception is that when we were saved, God forgave only those sins we had committed up to that point. Then through confession, we keep our salvation "up to date." If that were true, we could have no assurance of heaven. What if you or I were to die tomorrow with unconfessed sins on our conscience? Would we be lost and headed for hell?

The good news is that when we trusted Christ as our Savior, in one act, God wiped all of our sins away—even the sins we have not yet committed. The text says He forgave us "*all* our trespasses" the moment we were saved. Those who have believed on Christ belong to Him forever. We are declared righteous by God because Christ's righteousness is credited to us. Yes, He already has wiped the whole slate clean; or better, He has thrown the slate away. "For by a single offering he has perfected for all time those who are being sanctified" (Heb. 10:14).

This explains why you, as a Christian, cannot commit the unpardonable sin. You have been given a *carte blanche* pardon.

There is therefore now no condemnation for those who are in Christ Jesus. (Rom. 8:1)

And again,

Who shall bring any charge against God's elect? It is God who justifies. Who is to condemn? Christ Jesus is the one who died—more than that, who was raised—who is at the right hand of God, who indeed is interceding for us. (Rom. 8:33–34)

At this point we must stop for a moment and catch our breath! God's grace is so overwhelming we might be tempted to misuse it. A better response would be to pause and thank God for His generosity—it prompted Him to accept us unconditionally into His family.

Quite naturally we might ask: If our future sins already have been forgiven by God, why must we confess our sins? John wrote to Christians, "If we confess our sins, he is faithful and just to forgive us our sins and to cleanse us from all unrighteousness" (1 John 1:9).

When I said that God has already forgiven our sins, I was speaking in a legal sense. Once the righteousness of Christ has been credited to us and God has stamped "Paid in Full" across our lives, we are secure in our Father's love. Legally, all of our sins are blotted out. We have been "accepted in the beloved" (Eph. 1:6 KJV). Now God wants our experience to be in line with our official standing, and confession is the means God uses to bring us back into fellowship with Him.

Confession, or repentance, is our lifelong responsibility as Christians; it is God's way of keeping us honest in fellowship with Him. The sins we commit as Christians can be compared to our disobedience as children. As I was growing up, I often disappointed my parents through my lack of submission to their authority. When I was disciplined for my disobedience, I did not lose my sonship— though my fellowship with them was broken. When I returned to them and asked forgiveness for my misdeeds, I received it.

God does the same with us. If we are not willing to repent of the sin that the Holy Spirit brings to our attention, He disciplines us by allowing us to be ensnared by the consequences of that particular sin. God has His way of correcting us if we flippantly misuse His grace. Yet our sonship is secure; our future with God is guaranteed. Twenty-four hours a day God demands perfect righteousness from us; twenty-four hours a day Christ is before the Father, representing us, supplying exactly what we need.

Many Christians are miserable simply because they are unwilling to admit their sin humbly before God so that their conscience might be cleansed. They do not have to be saved again; they are just wayward children who need to get back on talking terms with their heavenly Father.

Let me assure you, it is God's desire for you to be totally free from guilt. Why should you continue to bear the condemnation of sins for which Christ has already paid? If Christ's death has allowed you to rejoice in your forgiveness, would you not best honor His sacrifice by accepting this gift with joy?

DIFFICULTIES IN ACCEPTING FORGIVENESS

Why do so many Christians find it difficult to really believe that God has forgiven them? The promises of God's forgiveness are clear, but accepting that forgiveness is another matter. Something within us says, "It's too good to be true." Such forgiveness seems to contradict the normal patterns of life. Let me suggest several reasons why some forgiven people still struggle with guilt.

The Consequences of Sin

First, the continued consequences of sin make it difficult to accept God's forgiveness. Think of a teenage girl, pregnant with a child out of wedlock. She confesses her sin, and it is forgiven, cleansed by the Most High God. Yet she is pregnant and soon will give birth. She finds it hard to accept forgiveness because the child is a reminder of her waywardness. She must learn to separate the *consequences* of sin from the *forgiveness* of sin. That is, she must realize that God forgives us for sins that have lingering, ongoing consequences in our lives and the lives of others.

The man who says he will not seek forgiveness for having given his wife AIDS but wants to burn in hell because he deserves it—that man must learn to separate forgiveness and consequences. Of course he deserves to burn in hell, just as all of us do! Yet he can be washed whiter than snow, even if his wife dies of the virus.

I am told that Ted Bundy, who died in the electric chair for killing approximately twenty-eight young women, accepted Christ as Savior before his death. We cannot verify this, for no one can know the human heart, but *it is possible that he did.* If so, he entered into the presence of God absolutely acquitted, forgiven, and cleansed by God—despite the awful continuing results of his hideous crimes.

Thankfully, God forgives sins whose consequences continue even into eternity. "As far as the east is from the west, so far does he remove our transgressions from us" (Ps. 103:12).

The Misunderstanding of Guilt

A second reason some people find it hard to accept God's forgiveness is that they view guilt as necessary punishment. I've counseled Christians who postponed confessing their sins, thinking it was just too easy to come to God and be instantly forgiven. Or, after confessing, they have continued to bear the guilt of their sin, insisting that they pay at least something to balance the scales. That is the devil's lie.

Guilt is not God's punishment! God uses guilt for one purpose only, and that is to lead us to Christ that we might repent of our sins and be cleansed. Guilt is God's way of reminding us we have violated His standard and must be brought back into moral agreement with Him.

Of course, we should feel guilty when we sin; not to feel guilt is a sign of a hard heart. But once we have confessed those sins, guilt has accomplished its purpose. It is never a means of payment, never a feeling we must endure because we deserve it. Such reasoning denies the liberating truth that Christ paid our price in full. Guilt cannot add a single stroke of merit to the perfect sacrifice. What makes us think that any good work we do could mean more to God than the work of His blessed Son? David, an adulterer and murderer, yet experienced the "joy" of his salvation (Ps. 51:12).

I've learned by experience that many Christians cannot distinguish the prompting of the Holy Spirit from the accusations of Satan. The difference is this: The Holy Spirit convicts us for sins that we have been unwilling to face in God's presence; Satan makes us feel guilty for sins that are already "under the blood of Christ," that is, for sins that we have already confessed. The Holy Spirit reminds us of our sins *before* we are cleansed; Satan continues to remind us of them *after* we are cleansed.

The Difficulty of Personal Forgiveness

A third reason we often struggle with accepting God's forgiveness is that *we cannot forgive ourselves.* We can understand that God is gracious and merciful, but we find it impossible to make peace with ourselves. A couple who gave up their child for adoption realized too late that the baby was accepted into the home of a family dedicated to a non-Christian religion. Humanly speaking, their child may never hear the gospel of Christ. Yes, God has forgiven them; but they cannot forgive themselves.

But if God—the one who knows all about us, the supreme Lawgiver of the universe—has forgiven His children, what right do we have to deny ourselves forgiveness? Do we know something about our lives that God has overlooked? If the Almighty has pronounced us clean, do we have the right to pronounce ourselves guilty?

When we say that we cannot forgive ourselves, we depreciate the value of Christ's sacrifice. The assumption is that we have come across a sin that was not included in Christ's death. Even the idea that we can help atone for our sin smacks of a strange kind of self-righteousness. In my counseling, I have discovered that most people who have never forgiven themselves have not really accepted God's forgiveness. To experience peace with God is to be at peace with oneself.

Returning to Habitual Sins

Finally, if you *intend to keep committing the same sin,* you will never feel forgiven, no matter how intense your confession. A man may confess his sexual infidelity to God, but unless he is willing to break with this sin entirely (this almost always involves seeking counsel and the forgiveness of those he has wronged), he will not sense the inner cleansing that comes with a cleansed conscience.

We find it so much easier to confess our sins to God than to make restitution. Yet when we come to God, we must be honest. Being willing to do whatever we can to be reconciled with those whom we have sinned against is absolutely essential for us in order to experience God's complete forgiveness.

Reconciliation can be difficult if the person we hurt or offended will not forgive us. In fact, we may be afraid of the other person's reaction, even wondering if reconciliation is worth the attempt. But we must do our best and leave the results to God. We must do our part even if our goodwill is not reciprocated. Paul delineates our responsibility: "Be kind to one another, tender-hearted, forgiving each other, just as God in Christ also has forgiven you" (Eph. 4:32). If we have wronged others, we must make sure we seek their forgiveness. Our goal is to have a conscience void of offense toward God and toward men (the subject of a future chapter).

In those instances where our actions have affected others, we especially need to have the courage to deal with our sins in the presence of some other human being(s). When James wrote, "Therefore, confess your sins to one another and pray for one another, that you may be healed" (James 5:16), he was not speaking about just the healing of the body, but also of the healing of the soul. Every one of us, at some time or another, must confront our past in the light of others and their response to us. We need to share our life with at least one other committed Christian who can understand the depths of our sin and yet can give us the assurance of Christ: "Neither do I condemn you; go, and from now on sin no more" (John 8:11).

There can be no growth in the Christian life until the barrier of guilt from the past has been cleared away.

LIVING WITH THE CONSEQUENCES

Okay, you have accepted God's forgiveness, and you have chosen to forgive yourself—but the consequences we have mentioned are still there, aren't they?

The mother who aborted her child knows she is forgiven, but how does she handle the memory of that precious little baby she killed? And what about this little one whom she will someday see in heaven—will that little girl ever understand? There are days when this young woman is able to push the thoughts out of her mind, but too often they crash back into her consciousness like a dam that has just broken.

A man looks back to a life of alcoholism that drove his children away from home. A husband faces the painful fact that his affair caused a divorce he did not want, and now he must live separated from his family. How do they handle these situations?

The only sensible course of action is to *give these consequences to God.* Some matters must be transferred from our hands to His. When we trust Him to make the best of the mess we have left behind, He will be gracious and display His mercy and grace. The forgiveness of God must be enjoyed even if reconciliation with the estranged person does not occur.

Adam and Eve, who made the biggest blunder known to man, were clothed by God with the skins of animals. David, who committed adultery with Uriah's wife, Bathsheba, married her and had a son with her named Solomon, whom "the Lord loved" (2 Sam. 12:24). As it is written: "Where sin increased, grace abounded all the more" (Rom. 5:20). Even weeds, growing as a result of the earth's curse, frequently are graced with beautiful flowers.

Thankfully, the doctrine of karma—that "unbreakable" impersonal law that says everyone gets exactly what he deserves—is a lie. The Bible assures us that God often curtails the consequences of sin, even in this life. Grace means we get what we don't deserve.

> He does not deal with us according to our sins, nor repay us according to our iniquities. For as high as the heavens are above the earth, so great is his steadfast love toward those who fear him. (Ps. 103:10–11)

God completely blots out our sins so that He no longer remembers them.

> I, I am he who blots out your transgressions for my own sake, and I will not remember your sins. (Isa. 43:25)

Does this mean He is no longer omniscient? Is there really something about us He does not know? Hardly. The text simply means that God no longer has regard for our sins. He does not remind us of them; they are no longer barriers to our fellowship with Him. Someone has said that He throws our sins into the sea and then puts up a sign that reads "No Fishing!"

Memories can be reminders of God's matchless grace. Of course the past sins will come to mind, but they need not control our future. God can break the power of these memories and eventually relegate them to the "no longer active" file of the mind. We just don't have a right to remember what God forgets.

In a subsequent chapter, we will discuss those deeper memories, the injustices done against another person—child abuse, for example—but what we must realize here is that God is greater than our memories.

REPAIRING THE IRREPARABLE

Satan has a vested interest in getting us to believe there are some sins for which there is no forgiveness. *The more he can magnify the horrors of our sin, the more he diminishes the value of Christ's death.* Of course, sin is destructive to man and abhorrent to God, but God's remedy is equal to the task. He took into account the full extent of human need when He accepted Christ's payment.

Recently, a friend sent me this story that illustrates God's forgiveness and the fact that Satan has no right to harass us about sins God has forgiven.

In the fourteenth century, Robert the Bruce of Scotland was leading his men in a battle to gain independence from England. Near the end of the conflict, the English wanted to capture Bruce to keep him from the Scottish crown. So they put his own bloodhounds on his trail. When the bloodhounds got close, Bruce could hear their baying. His attendant said, "We are done for. They are on your trail, and they will reveal your hiding place."

Bruce replied, "It's all right." Then he headed for a stream that flowed through the forest. He plunged in and waded upstream a short distance. When he came out on the other bank, he was in the depths of the forest. Within minutes, the hounds, tracing their master's steps, came to the bank. They went no farther. The English soldiers urged them on, but the trail was broken. The stream had carried the scent away. A short time later, the crown of Scotland rested on the head of Robert the Bruce.

The memory of our sins, prodded by Satan, can be like those baying dogs—but a stream flows, red with the blood of God's own Son. By grace, through faith, we are safe. No sin-hound can touch us. The trail is broken by the precious blood of Christ. I shall repeat: *There is more grace in God's heart than there is sin in our past.*

"The purpose of the Cross," someone observed, "is to repair the irreparable."

ACTION STEP

Thank God that Christ died for the greatest of sinners; yes, even criminals. Receive the cleansing and forgiveness promised to those who put faith in Him.

Memorize Psalm 32, written by David after he was forgiven for adultery and murder. Stay in prayer until your conscience has been cleansed by God. Ask God to show you steps to take toward those with whom you should seek reconciliation.

Chapter 4

Confronting
Fatal Addictions

R ichard Brzeczek made it to the top very fast," wrote Cheryl
Lavin in the *Chicago Tribune,* but "he made it to the bottom
even faster."[10]

Brzeczek, who was the superintendent of the Chicago Police Department, blew it all in four short years. "By the time he was 42 he had been in and out of two psychiatric hospitals," had been humiliated in a run for Cook County state's attorney, and had become an alcoholic and a victim of deep depression. To add to his guilt and misery, he had two affairs and was, in his words, "addicted to adultery."

Sexual addiction is the phrase making the rounds in counseling rooms and mental institutions. This is the recognition that it is possible to become so powerless against sexual temptation that the sufferer gives in to it repeatedly, despite the guilt, depression, and deceit accompanying such actions.

In Proverbs, we read about the person who is like a city without walls. Quite literally, he has no defenses; he succumbs to temptation without a fight—or if he does fight, he always loses.

In his book *Addicted to Adultery: How We Saved Our Marriage/ How You Can Save Yours,*[11] Richard Brzeczek and his wife tell the story of how affairs begin and how they end. They also give insight into the nature of sexual addiction.

Brzeczek's first affair began innocently enough. A flight attendant sat next to him during a trip to Washington. "From the moment she sat down next to me, there were certain silent messages between us . . . an electricity . . . a physical enticement that was new, exciting, and very stimulating."

Though he loved his wife and was not looking for an affair, he and this woman, whom he calls Diane, shared some lunches and then a hotel room. The affair turned into an obsession. "It was like a fix," he recalled. "For me to make a phone call to her was the equivalent of a junkie shooting up some heroin. If I didn't make the contact, I'd be hysterical. It was like withdrawal. I would be crying, sobbing uncontrollably."[12]

Along with his obsession with Diane, he also became hooked on danger. He knew he could be caught, yet he took risks. He even found lying addictive. When he was deceptive, the adrenaline rushed through him as he fabricated more stories and took even greater risks. He began a second affair and enjoyed the euphoria of seeing two mistresses without either knowing of the other.

When confronted with the evidence, he lied to his wife and to his marriage counselor and his therapist. "I actually had the doctors convinced that I wasn't the one with the problem, but Liz was."[13] In retrospect, he wonders how he kept all of the lies straight while he was talking to three different women. "The stress of trying to remember what I told to whom was about to kill me. I'm surprised I didn't have a heart attack."[14]

Brzeczek began to drink more heavily, and this increased his guilt and depression. After he finally told his wife about the affairs, he promised to end the relationships. Yet that same day, he promised

Diane he would marry her. During his political campaign, he often would have to cancel meetings because he was either intoxicated or depressed. The pressure was turned up a notch when he discovered he was being investigated for dipping into the police contingency fund. Little wonder he lost the race for state's attorney to his opponent, Richard M. Daley.

Despite his intention to reform, the lying continued. He kept lying to his wife, children, and friends. Of course, he lied to himself, too. Deviously manipulating so many people and seeing what all this was doing to his family made it almost impossible for him to look at himself in the mirror each morning.

During "the next several months, he lost all control over his life. He stopped shaving and showering and changing his clothes." He would phone his girlfriend in front of his wife and kids, begging her to come and be with him. He felt paralyzed and depressed. He would lie on the couch and drink—and cry. He contemplated suicide.

Richard Brzeczek says he "found God in a psychiatric ward, where he stayed for over a month." He credits God and his psychiatrist for "the strength to break up with Diane." That was the beginning of the healing process. His marriage was saved despite the fact that on the day of his release, he was indicted on "24 counts of theft and official misconduct." He was later acquitted of the charges.[15]

The Brzeczeks worked through their pain and spent the rest of their married lives helping other couples save their marriages. Their book is an honest account of the power of an adulterous relationship. Yes, there is such a thing as addiction to adultery.

Later in this book, sexuality will be discussed in more detail. Sexual sins are always at the top of any list of the most powerful temptations. We must understand the power of sexual bonding and the special effects of illicit sexual experiences. In this chapter, we shall consider addictions in general so that we have an understanding of both their source and power. Best of all, we will look at the Scriptures to be reminded that there is a way out.

THE SOURCE AND POWER OF ADDICTION

Addiction. The word refers to compulsive behaviors that could control any of us. We all know about the power of alcohol, drugs, and gambling, but today we also hear about workaholics and, of course, sex addicts. Some people are addicted to pornography; others, to overeating.

Although addicts have existed since the beginning of the human race, their number now appears to be on the increase. The availability of drugs and pornography and the legalization of gambling all contribute to this escalation of addictive behavior.

More important, the breakup of the family provides the soil in which addictions can grow quickly. Powerful compulsions often can be traced to a dysfunctional family history—indeed, addictions have been in some family lines for generations. In *Out of the Shadows: Understanding Sexual Addiction,* Patrick Carnes writes: "Sexual compulsiveness, like all addictions, rests in a complex web of family relationships."[16]

There are at least two ways of viewing addiction: as a disease or as a sin. Some groups have labeled addiction a disease, hoping this will make it easier for the sufferer to seek help. Just as there is no reason to be ashamed of having measles or a gallstone, they say, so there is no shame in having the disease of alcoholism or sexual compulsiveness.

The downside to this approach is that it makes the cure more difficult, since the addict believes he bears no responsibility for catching the "disease." Let us be honest enough to admit that addiction is nothing more than what J. Keith Miller has rightly called the "blinding self-absorption called sin." He continues, "Sin is the universal addiction to self that develops when individuals put themselves in the center of their personal world in a way that leads to abuse of others or self. Sin causes sinners to seek instant gratification, to be first, and to get more than their share—now."[17]

In light of this, addicts must realize that Christ has not promised to heal all of our diseases this side of heaven, but He has promised to deliver us from our sins. If approached through Christ, God has always promised to come to the aid of sinners who seek His forgiveness and help.

In the following pages I shall answer, from a biblical perspective, several common questions about addiction:

- What are the steps that lead to addiction?
- What are the chains that keep a person bound?
- And, finally, what are the keys—the principles—that can break the vicious cycle?

STEPS THAT LEAD TO ADDICTION

In Romans 1, Paul gives a spiritual history of the human race, detailing the origin of many kinds of sins and addictions of which homosexuality is one. However, a person who ends up in any of these sinful lifestyles or addictions may be totally unaware of the process Paul outlines here. Paul's lists are applicable to all other sins and addictions. Proof that we should give his words a wider interpretation is given in verses 28–32; there he lists a total of twenty-two sins that grow out of the spiritual decline of the human race.

Read this descending staircase that bottoms out in the wasteland of addiction, violence, and perversion:

> For although they knew God, they did not honor him as God or give thanks to him, but they became futile in their thinking, and their foolish hearts were darkened. Claiming to be wise, they became fools, and exchanged the glory of the immortal God for images resembling mortal man and birds

and animals and creeping things. Therefore God gave them up in the lusts of their hearts. (Rom. 1:21–24)

People began by dishonoring God through failing even to recognize the creature/Creator distinction, which often breeds anger toward God and a callous disregard for His authority. Next comes hard-heartedness and a determination to tune God out of one's life and existence. What happened when God was not given His rightful place?

Step #1: The True God Was Replaced with a False God

We are spiritual creatures, so we cannot live in a spiritual vacuum. For a man to live without a god is like a fish trying to live without water. Therefore, when the true God is abandoned, another will be substituted. Just name an addict's addiction and you have named his god.

Step #2: The Truth of God Was Changed into a Lie

God created us in such a way that it is difficult for us to violate what we know to be true. So in the interest of fulfilling our desires, we are prone to rationalize our behavior. The only way this can be done is to call God's truth a lie.

All addicts change the truth of God into a lie. We've already learned that alcoholics and adulterers lie to other people and, more seriously, lie to themselves. They either tell themselves there is nothing wrong with their behavior, or they blame others for what they are doing, or they assure themselves that they are in full control of their particular vice. They are not addicted, and they can stop whenever they like. Besides, they have every right to live as they do.

This explains why addictions involve so much denial—nobody can practice destructive behavior without exchanging truth for lies. Truth and wholesome behavior are inseparably linked. When God's restraints are thrown off, truth must also be jettisoned.

Step #3: The God-Given Natural Functions Were Exchanged for Unnatural Ones

We all have basic needs that cry for fulfillment. When we "take control of our lives," we tell ourselves we have every right to meet our needs without reference to God.

Addiction is nothing more than trying to meet legitimate needs in illegitimate ways. When a man squeezes God out of his thoughts, he ends up making many vain attempts to deaden the pain of an empty life. Any one of a number of sins can become a root addiction (Rom. 1:28–32). We should not be surprised at multiple addictions—people running from one compulsion to another or involved with several at the same time. Addiction is a crutch, man's substitute for God-centered living.

Most of the human race suffers from some kind of addiction. To be free from sin's power is the exception rather than the rule. You do not have to have a perverse streak of evil to become an addict. Addicts can be everyday people—people you work with, people you go to church with, people you live with. An addict can be anyone taking the path of least resistance, pursuing his innate desires with abandon.

Addiction is a continuum, not a hardened absolute state. Some addicts are under the power of sin more than others, but everyone bears God's image. A consummate addict is one who has taken a few more wrong turns than his neighbor—assuming his neighbor isn't a consummate addict, too.

Think of your life as a car with you at the wheel. An addict is simply someone who has lost control. His hand is on the steering wheel, but the steering column is disconnected from the front wheels. He has only the illusion of control.

In the previous chapter, I referred to Ted Bundy, the criminal who confessed to killing twenty-eight girls and young women. He began reading pornography at a young age. As the excitement of this wore off, he sought to re-create the same euphoria he had originally experienced. He imagined what it would be like to molest a child; then he had to act it out to see if the experience was as great as he imagined. Then he visualized strangling a child, to see if this would give him an even greater erotic experience.

After his first strangulation, he said he could hardly believe he was capable of such an awful crime. Nevertheless, he craved to reach the same euphoric experience again and again—so the murders continued. He became a consummate addict.

Thankfully, only a small percentage of pornography addicts go on to such crimes. But once you relinquish the control of your life to an addiction, once the steering wheel is disconnected, it is no longer you who decides where the car will go. Not everyone who loses control lands in the same place. Some drive into a ditch and have a few bruises; others tumble into a valley and are permanently wounded; still others hit an oncoming car and innocent people are maimed or killed.

Like these errant drivers, every so often an addict experiences a "near miss." The gay person thinks they contracted an STD, the alcoholic is fired from their job, and the adulterer fears his wife will discover his affair; the child molester is terrified that they might have been seen, and the gambler is tossed out of their apartment because they blew their money. These people swear they will quit their destructive behavior, and many of them do—for a time.

Successful as these interludes may be, they only give an illusion of control. Usually, such modifications of behavior are only preludes to more daring adventures. Soon the addict is back to the guilt-ridden cycle. I'm reminded of Mark Twain's cynical remark, "Of course I can quit smoking. I've done it a thousand times!"

Why is their reform short-lived? They have not been willing to face the pain of self-evaluation or the issues they will have to deal with in reestablishing contact with God and others who can help them. Addicts have been known to lie, cheat, manipulate, shift blame, steal, and make others feel guilty for their problems. The denial game all over again.

CHAINS THAT KEEP ADDICTS BOUND

Why is it so hard to walk away from an addiction? Why not just wake up some morning and say, "Enough is enough!" and leave it all behind?

Powerful, secret chains will not let the addict be free. He has allowed those chains to become strong, and now he no longer contests their power.

What are those secret chains?

Chain #1: Guilt and Shame

The addict is constantly violating his own moral standards. He knows that what he is doing contradicts his upbringing and standards of decency. He also knows that he is hurting himself and others, but he continues the difficult task of a double existence—one life in his family and society, the other in his world of addiction.

Even more threatening is the fact that he knows that God sees his every move. His hypocrisy tears at him, for he is secretly aware that he is but a human shell. He cannot afford to be honest, for then the game would be over. He must lie to others and to himself. The guilt and shame become excruciating, but he sees no other way. He continues to be torn apart, part of him wanting to be free, another part believing life without his addiction would be unbearable.

Chain #2: Dishonesty

Fear of exposure is so painful that, even when he is discovered, he evades the truth. The smart addict has readied himself for just such a moment. He has spent hours arming himself with a pack of lies he can use at any moment. Since the addict's whole life is a lie, telling several more is of no great moral significance.

The more he lies, the greater his guilt and shame. Even when he decides to "come clean," he will usually tell only part of the story. Dishonesty is another of his many crutches.

Chain #3: Euphoria

No one can calculate the number of hours the addict spends trying to work out schemes that will give him the euphoria he seeks. Just planning his next move brings a rush of excitement.

The addict thinks no one else has ever experienced the intense pleasure he receives through his addiction. *No one,* he thinks, *can understand the elation and satisfaction that can come from pornography, alcohol, or drugs.* If he is addicted to gambling, he is driven by the euphoria of taking a risk, of making a bet. These impassioned sensations are his very own, and no one can take them from him.

Life without these pleasurable sensations seems unbearable. All of his psychic energy is spent trying to figure out how to make sure nothing will ever come between him and his beautiful feeling. The alcoholic is obsessed with making sure he will always have his supply of alcohol, no matter what. The voyeur is consumed with the rush of pleasure that comes when he sees a partially clad woman through a bedroom window. Just the anticipation stimulates him. He will spend hours in the dark waiting for a few fleeting seconds of erotica. He becomes a slave to the waves of sensation that pulse through his body. The tycoon on Wall Street who already has a hundred million dollars but cheats to get more is addicted to "the deal." That is his shot of heroin. He is consumed with greed and the power it brings. Wielding such power becomes his fix.

This ought to be a warning to never become involved in addictive behavior. Those first steps may create within us sensations we will want repeated over and over again. It is better never to have experienced the exhilaration of alcohol, drugs, pornography, or adultery. No one ever begins along these paths with the intention of becoming an addict. Everyone thinks that he or she has this bit of pleasure under control.

Chain #4: Fear of Rejection

The addict wants to seek help, but he cannot bear to do so for fear he would be rejected or despised. He has the emotional need to be accepted as a person with value and with the potential for a better life.

He is, to use a phrase, caught between a rock and a hard place. If he tells his story, he fears rejection. Yet the only way for him to get out of his prison is to share his need with a fellow human being. Alcoholics Anonymous is successful because one of the most powerful forces for transformation is honest interaction with other people who are fighting the same battles. That's why we have so many other "anonymous" groups today—sex addicts, gamblers, overeaters. The addict says, "Finally I've found someone who understands my struggle, and he can't reject me because he's in the same predicament I am!"

Possibly these groups had to begin outside the established church because too many people felt they could never be honest in church; everyone else seemed to be above the battle. Thankfully, the church is changing, as many are beginning ministries like Celebrate Recovery for those who struggle with sinful habits.

Chain #5: Loneliness

Addicts lonely? Perhaps a distraught wife says, "No, that can't be true. My husband was an alcoholic, and he wasn't lonely at all—in fact, I bore him ten children."

But, in truth, addicts usually end up withdrawing from society, satisfied with only the minimal interaction needed for everyday living. Eventually, they also withdraw from their families, brooding alone about their problems and their next "fix."

When their inner pain seems to be unbearable, they often resort to violent behavior. An addict of any type may abuse his wife, beat his children, and display many other forms of irrational hostility. As we have learned, he shifts the blame for his behavior to others, for he cannot bear to admit the truth. But he feels lonely because he thinks that no one really understands him.

Chain #6: Sense of Worthlessness

Addictions often develop as a result of the pain caused by dysfunctional family relationships. Sometimes the roots of addiction even span generations. If you were abused, you will have a greater propensity to escape from your pain in self-defeating, compulsive, addictive behavior. If you were thrown onto the street at a young age, you will have a much stronger tendency to deaden the pain by seeking the cheap thrills of pornography, alcoholism, drugs, or sex. Eventually, these will become the crutches you use to cope with reality. The addictions become your god—only *they* can get you from point A to point B. You fear life without your crutch.

Call it what you will, addicts live in an emotional vacuum. They have deep needs they are trying to meet. Unfortunately, they do this in ways that will leave them with even deeper needs. Like men drifting helplessly in a boat on a saltwater sea, the more they drink to slake their thirst, the thirstier they become.

Understandably, such people have a feeling of worthlessness, an abandonment to the monotonous routine of daily living. Even when a person like this has a job, his favorite addiction is never far from his mind. The alcoholic drinks to overcome the problems caused by his alcoholism, and the sex addict opts for a series of sexual encounters to hide the pain caused by his immorality. The gambler makes bets to try to cover the losses incurred by his gambling. Change seems impossible.

KEYS TO UNLOCK THE PRISONS

Addictions have been around since the fall of man in Eden. The church in Corinth was trying to survive in a culture inundated with immoral addictions. Just up the hill was a temple dedicated to prostitution. One thousand free prostitutes were available for the populace. Every form of sexual sin was practiced without shame or inhibition.

Converts out of that culture brought with them the struggles we are so familiar with today. Some new believers wanted to legitimize their behavior; they wanted to bend the rules so they could feel comfortable without giving up their cherished pleasures. To these Paul wrote:

> Or do you not know that the unrighteous will not inherit the kingdom of God? Do not be deceived: neither the sexually immoral, nor idolaters, nor adulterers, nor men who practice homosexuality, nor thieves, nor the greedy, nor drunkards, nor revilers, nor swindlers will inherit the kingdom of God. And such were some of you. But you were washed, you were sanctified, you were justified in the name of the Lord Jesus Christ and by the Spirit of our God. (1 Cor. 6:9–11)

Name your addiction, and Paul mentions it, at least in its root form. Yet he also says this was the *past* experience of believers and not their present disposition.

Those in spiritual slavery would not inherit the kingdom. Some scholars say that this is a description of the unconverted; others believe that Paul is referring to those who are true Christians but whose lifestyle forbids them the privilege of ruling with Christ in the kingdom which they nevertheless will be allowed to enter. One thing is certain: God does not excuse their behavior or trivialize it with euphemisms.

Three words in 1 Corinthians 6:11 describe the keys, or principles, that free a person from the enslaving power of addictions: *washed, sanctified,* and *justified.* Scholars are puzzled as to why the sequence seems to be backwards—we would say justification is first. But Paul is simply beginning with the individual's experience and working back to the basis of it.

Key #1: Washed—Forgiven

This means that the guilt and shame that bound these believers was taken away. We've all used a water hose to wash a gutter clean. When God applies His cleansing, the pollution of the conscience can be made clean.

Think of what this means to the addict—to have all the guilt and shame rinsed away! No longer a voice of condemnation, no longer the feelings of hypocrisy and self-incrimination. Cleansed!

Sometimes we need others to confirm that we have been forgiven by God. We can be helped in the process by the instruction of pastors and teachers who have been given to the church. Yes, God has forgiven us, but the body of Christ can help make that real to us.

Key #2: Sanctified—Set Apart

The word *sanctified* has the same root as the word *holy.* This means that we are special to God; we are not ordinary but extraordinary. I know an artist who is so in love with a particular picture that he built a special wall for it in his new home. If that picture were a person, he would know he is very special to his owner.

We have been set apart by God for special treatment. The person who comes to Christ, regardless of his past, is assured a place of prominence. Yes, there is a purpose for living; yes, God is not finished with us yet.

Key #3: Justified—Accepted

We studied forgiveness in the preceding chapter. Here we remind ourselves that despite their past behavior, God declared the believers in Corinth to be as righteous as Christ. That's what justification means. Every person justified by God receives the same righteousness, without distinction. The gay person, the alcoholic, and the adulterer all have the same acceptance and privilege before God as the person who has escaped all these sins.

Think of what this means to the addict—they can be number one on God's list of things to take care of in the universe! This is the beginning of freedom from the chains that bind. Receiving the gift of eternal life through Christ is the doorway, the first step in the walk to freedom. They must begin by knowing that they belong to God, that they have been cleansed by Him. The shackles of guilt and shame must be broken.

The first step listed by Alcoholics Anonymous is the humble acknowledgment that you cannot fight this battle on your own. It is not, however, up to us to choose whatever "higher power" we wish; we must choose the one and only God and Father of our Lord Jesus Christ, for only He can wash, sanctify, and justify us.

Accountability is necessary for those who wish to be free from the power of addiction. So necessary is it, that without an honest relationship with a counselor/mentor, the chains cannot be broken.

REASONS TO STAY FREE AND PURE

Is that the end of the struggle? No, because you need to face the conditions and struggles that led you into the addiction in the first place. This is when the body of Christ needs to step in, help fill the emotional vacuum, and provide support and encouragement to the addict in his battle for a pure life.

Paul gives three reasons why the believers in Corinth should live sexually pure lives. All three members of the Trinity play a role in our salvation; thus God can free us from addictions of any sort. God becomes our ally in the fight for personal purity and freedom.

Reason #1: We Are Joined to Christ

"Do you not know that your bodies are members of Christ?" (1 Cor. 6:15). This fact gives us the right to break all obligations to our addiction. Our bond to Christ is stronger than our bond to destructive behavior. If you are a part of Christ, and I am a part of Christ, then we are joined to each other. If God has washed, sanctified, and justified you, we must join one another in the battle for freedom in Christ.

Every one of us needs at least one prayer partner, one person who loves us enough to give both rebuke and encouragement. Just as the physical body has the power to heal itself when the skin has been punctured, so Christ's body also has the resources to take the wounded part and make it whole.

When I stumble on a sidewalk, my hands instinctively reach out to absorb the blow to my head. My wrists are willing to be broken for the sake of other parts of my body. When the body of Christ begins to live like our physical bodies, the weaker parts are strengthened.

Reason #2: We Are Indwelt by the Holy Spirit

"Do you not know that your body is a temple of the Holy Spirit within you, whom you have from God? You are not your own" (1 Cor. 6:19). In the Old Testament there were two parts to the temple: the outer court (the temple area) and the inner sanctuary where God dwelt (the Holy of Holies). The Greek word Paul uses here is *naos,* which means the "inner shrine." In practical terms, this means that the Holy of Holies has been transferred to our human bodies. God dwells within us.

Therefore, the addict has the possibility of emotional healing. That "hole in the soul" that fuels the addiction can be filled with wholeness. The loneliness, guilt, and shame can be replaced by what the Holy Spirit is committed to bring to our lives, namely, emotional and spiritual strength.

The work of the Spirit is so wholesome, so fulfilling, that He substitutes for the euphoria created by the addictions we have talked about. It is peace without guilt and love without bitterness. That's why Paul says, "Do not get drunk with wine, for that is debauchery, but be filled with the Spirit" (Eph. 5:18).

Reason #3: We Belong to God

"For you were bought with a price. So glorify God in your body" (1 Cor. 6:20). Here we have the answer to our sense of worthlessness. The God of the universe purchased us at high cost. We belong to His family. Whatever our background, whatever hurts have been created by our human family, God can heal them by giving us a new identity.

I do not want to hold out the promise that your addictions will immediately disappear, although I do know of some people who were delivered instantly by Christ. More realistically, I believe the inner work of God in the soul is so sure and so steady that eventually the addiction drops away like dead leaves to make way for new life.

GROWING WITHIN

Overcoming the power of temptation is no small matter, especially if your struggle is long-standing. In fact, the propensity to return to your former lifestyle will always be there. Even when we are sincere in our commitment to Christ, the power of the flesh, strengthened by Satan, battles within us. There is no one act on your part—no act of repentance or promise you can make—that will guarantee your freedom.

The Christian life is one of growth through discipline, fellowship with other Christians, and accountability. Some behavioral ruts are intolerably deep, the patterns of the past unbearable. Understanding what Christ has done for us is the first step.

We are most vulnerable to sexual sins. And because they are different from all others, later chapters in this book will deal with sexuality in more detail. For now, it is sufficient to say that Christ invites us to enjoy His cleansing and submit to His authority. The road back might be long, but you can't begin the journey without taking that first big step.

Thousands can say there is life after addiction.

ACTION STEP

Pray that you will find one person with whom you can share your addiction, someone who will respect your confidentiality, accept you despite your guarded secret, and meet with you for prayer and counsel. Do not give up on your search. When your dark side is exposed to the light, your addiction will lose its power.

Chapter 5

The Hurt and Healing of Abuse

Feel the pain of the woman who wrote this letter to Ann Landers:

> My father, an alcoholic, began to abuse me when I was five years old. I finally found the courage to tell my mother five years later. She called me a liar and a troublemaker. After several weeks of my pleading and crying, throwing up, and having nightmares, she said, "I will leave it up to you. I will go to the police if you want me to, but they will put your father in jail and we will all probably starve to death."
>
> Being an insecure, emotionally troubled 10-year-old, I could not face that burden, so I chose to let the abuse go on. A year later, my father stopped abusing me and began to abuse my 5 and 7-year-old cousins who were living with us at the time.
>
> He died when I was 28. I did not cry at his funeral. My mother died nine years later, and I cried hysterically at hers—and every day after that for several weeks.
>
> I went for counseling and learned that I forgave my father because I came to understand that he was a sick man,

but I could not forgive my mother because she didn't protect me against him.

My relationships with men have been awful. My drug of choice was food. I am now in a 12-step program and getting better. Ann, please keep telling people who have been abused that silence is deadly. They must talk about it and get it out in the open. Only then will the healing begin.

P. J. in West Hartford[18]

Nothing is more deserving of tears than the plight of children in our society. Who can begin to count the buckets of tears that have been shed by children (and adults) who have been abused by those who should have loved them the most?

Thousands of adults languish in emotional distress, unable to make peace with the trauma of their childhood. To put such a past behind them is difficult; thankfully, God is able to make the pain bearable.

Abuse can take different forms. One is verbal abuse. Some parents call children names, predict future failure, and severely criticize them. Let's not think this abuse is not painful. There are thousands of people who can scarcely function because of destructive words still lodged like arrows in their souls.

A well-known singer whose father berated her as a child cannot even now overcome the emotional roadblocks erected by those harsh, uncaring words. To quote her, "Though a thousand people tell me I sing well, I cannot believe them, for the little girl in me still asks, 'If they are speaking the truth, why did my daddy tell his little girl she couldn't sing?' Something inside me says my daddy could not be wrong."

Though her daddy has been dead for many years, this woman says, "I want to be emotionally whole, but my daddy stands in the way." The power of verbal abuse.

Add to this the ugly reality of physical abuse. I shall not retell the stories that appear almost daily in the news: children locked in closets, beaten mercilessly, tied to bedposts, drowned in bathtubs. If just speaking of these atrocities causes us pain, imagine what it is like for the children who actually endure them.

Sexual abuse is also rampant throughout the land. A father molests his daughters; brothers and sisters are involved in various levels of experimentation. We've all heard the allegations against some schools and day care centers. And that is not to speak of what some babysitters have done.

Incredibly, one out of every five baby girls born this year will eventually be sexually molested by somebody, likely a member of her family, a relative, or a trusted friend.[19] In fact, sexual abuse occurs in all kinds of homes, Christian and non-Christian, rich and poor, educated and uneducated.

How many abusers are there in the world? We don't know, of course, but some have molested hundreds of children. Others just one or two. We do know their numbers are increasing.

SPECIAL PROBLEMS OF THE ABUSED

What are the special problems experienced by those who suffer such childhood trauma?

Intense Anger

Walk a mile in the sandals of those who have been abused. Yes, they may be adults now, but part of their life is missing. Somebody has stolen their happiness. It's not just because they remember the pain of the past, but it is also that the emotional paralysis does not allow them to function very well in the present.

Thanks to the abusers, these victims may now be unable to love, to trust, or to relate with others in freedom. They also may fail repeatedly in their activities, believing they are programmed for defeat.

What makes matters worse, the abuser likely got away with it; he is unpunished and totally unconcerned about the pain he inflicted. He may simply go from victim to victim without a twinge of conscience. Understandably, his victims are filled with resentment. These victims also may be angry with God. When I urged one woman to find healing for the abuse she suffered, she asked the troubling question referred to earlier in chapter 1: "God wasn't there for me when I was a child; why should I think He will be there for me as an adult? *I can never trust Him!*"

Victims of abuse are often angry—very angry. This may result in depression and anxiety.

Don't be quick to judge. How would you feel if someone you trusted stole your childhood? Anger is understandable.

The Bondage of Shame

Children have an innate respect for those two people who gave them life. They not only think that Father and Mother can do no wrong, but they crave the acceptance and love of their parents. When a parent abuses a child, the child believes he is getting his just deserts. To his way of thinking he is just as bad as his parents have made him out to be. Justice, children believe, is being served. This explains why a woman who has been abused by her father may seek to marry a man who will continue to abuse her. In effect she is saying, "I deserve to be abused, so I need to find someone who will give me what I deserve."

Many parents who abuse their children were themselves abused as children. A child who has been sexually abused feels dirty, unworthy, and ashamed. One abused woman said she felt as if the words *Damaged Goods* were written on her forehead. *No one,* she thought, *could possibly love me.*

Such a woman might follow through with what is called the "battered woman syndrome," seeking immoral relationships and even prostitution. Others become passive victims, looking for someone to abuse them. They live out the dark stain that smudges their soul. Some, thankfully, become emotionally whole.

Abusers have a way of making their captors feel guilty. A father may lead his daughter to believe she is a coconspirator, an accomplice in what happened. And, of course, since we are sexual creatures, a child may eventually enjoy the sexual sensations of the abuse. All of this combines to compound the guilt.

Difficulty in Establishing Deep Relationships

Those who have been abused find it difficult to trust others— they become fearful if a relationship becomes too personal and intimate. It is very common for victims to sabotage the very relationships they so desperately need. Those who have been rejected tend to act in such a way as to insure more rejection.

The abused often have two unconscious agendas. First, they feel the need to prove that no one is trustworthy. Having been betrayed by the person who should have protected them, they are convinced that all men (or women) are the same. Thus, they will become critical and suspicious, attitudes symptomatic of their distrust.

Second, they will try to prove that no one can love them. After all, they perceive themselves as unworthy of love, and they believe that all love is conditional. It is not uncommon for them to test every relationship to the limit, to make impossible demands on those who befriend them, insisting that someone else is responsible to make them happy. When their friends pull away from the relationship, they feel they have proven their point, and they exclaim, "See? Nobody really loves me!"

In a marriage relationship, the problem becomes excruciating. The formerly abused partner is impossible to please. By becoming critical and angry, clinging to unreasonable expectations, the victim inevitably makes life impossible. Intimacy becomes a threat to the abused partner, who does not feel loved but "used." Because a close relationship is nigh impossible, the marriage is soon in deep trouble.

As David Seamands wrote in *The Healing of Memories,* "When painful memories have not been faced, healed, and integrated into life, they often break through defenses and interfere with normal living.[20]

Those of us who were not abused must be patient with these victims. Our greatest contribution is to assure them of our love and acceptance, no matter what story they tell us about their past. On the other hand, we must also be aware of the games that are being played; we must not allow them to manipulate us with guilt. Sometimes there has to be loving but firm confrontation. Yes, love must sometimes be tough.

Most important, we can give them hope. We can assure them that there is life after abuse. Thousands have changed their status from victim to survivor.

If this sounds impossible, remember that it is exactly what Christ offers—a life that is supernatural. Resources are available for this transformation.

CHRIST, THE HEALER OF BROKEN HEARTS

Specifically, what can Christ do for those who hurt? One day He went into a synagogue in Nazareth and took down a scroll, turned to a few paragraphs in Isaiah, and read them. When He was finished He said, "Today this Scripture has been fulfilled in your hearing" (Luke 4:21).

This passage speaks of Christ's ability to deliver His people from captivity, the power He uses to free prisoners. It speaks of Christ as the Physician of the soul. The Isaiah passage reads:

The Spirit of the Lord GOD is upon me,
because the Lord has anointed me
to bring good news to the poor;
he has sent me to bind up the brokenhearted,
to proclaim liberty to the captives

and the opening of the prison to those who are bound;
to proclaim the year of the LORD's favor,
and the day of vengeance of our God;
to comfort all who mourn;
to grant to those who mourn in Zion—
to give them a beautiful headdress instead of ashes,
the oil of gladness instead of mourning,
the garment of praise instead of a faint spirit;
that they may be called oaks of righteousness,
the planting of the LORD, that he may be glorified.
(Isa. 61:1–3)

The Jews had been hauled off to Babylon by the thousands because of their persistent idolatry. There they wept, longing for the day when they could return to Jerusalem. Here the prophet writes about Christ, who would eventually deliver them. The context refers to literal, political fulfillment.

Yet Christ's use of this prophecy in Luke 4 gives us permission to apply the passage spiritually. He came to release us from any prison that will keep us from spiritual freedom.

He has been anointed to bring good news to the afflicted and to "bind up the brokenhearted." We usually think of binding up a broken arm, not a broken heart. But just as setting a broken bone helps it heal correctly, so Christ sets a broken heart so that it will heal to the best of its ability. The heart will still have a scar, but, spiritually speaking, it will be functional; it will not have a gaping wound. At least some healing will have taken place.

How does Christ do this for His people?

Christ Frees You from Your Captor

Your captor is anyone who has destructive authority over you. Christ came to set us free from those spiritual and emotional prisons others have built for us. He came to open the gates of the cell so we can walk out.

Who is the person who stole your childhood, who callously refused to hear your sobs, and who betrayed your trust? Christ can break his or her authority over you.

Perhaps you need to be free from the destructive power of your parents. God put it within the heart of every child to desire a father and mother who love him or her. Parents are to protect their children and give them the security needed to develop into responsible adults. The deepest hurt a child can have is not the death of a father or mother, but the betrayal of one or both of them. Verbal, physical, or sexual abuse from a parent—who should be giving love to his child—creates a raw wound of sorrow and pain.

Recently I spoke to a man who is so emotionally numb that he lives without feelings. He was raised by an irrational, paranoid mother who abused him physically and verbally. She called him names, assuring him that he would always be a failure, "just like his father." She hated all men in general and her husband in particular, and she vented this hatred upon her son. He told me, "You must understand that for me to succeed in my mother's eyes is to fail, for the only dream she ever had for me was failure. To this day, I can still hear her curses in my ears."

I was moved to put my hand on his shoulder and pray for him, trusting God to break all the negative influence his mother ever had on him. I helped him understand that some of the effects of his background would probably always be with him. Being at peace emotionally should not be his primary objective. What he must do is pursue God with all of his heart and soul. In other words, he must learn to become a worshiper now, not waiting until his past is resolved. God often uses hurt to cause us to seek Him with more intensity. Slowly this man is being led out of the prison built by an angry, uncaring woman he called "Mother."

Yes, we must honor our father and mother, but no child should be bound by a parent's madness. We esteem their position, but there are times when we must respectfully smash all of their misused authority in our lives. The influence of abusive parents must be broken, whether they are dead or alive.

Perhaps your captor is a sexual partner. A fine Christian girl refused to respond to the overtures of an older, immoral man. One day in exasperation, he raped her. Despite the humiliation and shame, the girl became his slave, willing to do whatever he asked. She actually became his voluntary prisoner.

Later in this book two chapters are devoted to those who struggle with past sexual experiences. Here it is sufficient to remember that there is a union formed during intercourse that has great emotional and spiritual implications. I call this a "soul-tie," which can be defined as a bond between two or more people that unites them in purpose, in desire, and in relationship. Such a tie is blessed by God in the marriage relationship between a man and a woman but becomes destructive outside of that relationship. Alien soul-ties breed guilt and distrust, searing images and memories within the mind that can only be broken through confession, renunciation, and the cleansing of Christ. A person who has had an immoral relationship must trust Christ to break the soul-tie that can keep that person imprisoned by his or her captor. Of course, breaking such a relationship is not always easy, for the captor may be able to cash in on a number of IOUs, such as the threat of exposure or other forms of blackmail.

If you are in such a situation, ask God to lead you to someone who can help you get free. The chains of tyrannical authority can be broken.

The most terrifying slavery I have ever seen was of a young woman I knew who came under the authority of a man with occult powers. He held her captive, forcing her to perform various kinds of unnatural and violent acts. He threatened her with death if she were to leave him, assuring her that she would be hunted and found. She was terrified and confused, not knowing where to turn. She both loved and hated him, unable to be out of his presence for more than a few hours. She was literally his slave.

Many cultists brainwash their captives so that they will even be willing to die for the leaders. These cultists bring the unwary under subjection to their authority under the guise of exercising legitimate spiritual leadership. Why don't the prisoners just leave? We ask that question only because we do not understand the awesome power a satanically inspired person can have over others. We do not understand soul-ties.

If you want your heart to be healed, you must come out from under the abusive authority of anyone who is evil, anyone who manipulates you or takes you captive. You are to be a slave only of Christ, not of your parents, nor of a friend turned enemy. You are not to be subject to some real or imagined person who has the power to program your soul.

What if you are married to such a person? What if there is abuse going on in your home now? You have the responsibility to share that information with someone who can help you. You must also realize that Christ can bring you out from under such a destructive influence. If you are faithful, He will do it in His own time and in His own way.

There are thousands of borderline cases, though, where control and abuse are not clearly differentiated. A wife lives as best she can with an alcoholic husband, and the children are mistreated only occasionally. Or a paranoid mother neglects her children or manipulates them with guilt. Abuse can take a thousand forms.

The negative effects of these influences must be broken; individuals must realize that the treatment they have endured is no measure of their worth. Christ can preserve the soul, providing hope even when the struggle rages.

There is a passage in *Uncle Tom's Cabin* in which a slave was being beaten, but "it was as if the blows fell only on his body, not his soul."

Yes, the soul is affected by what happens to us, but God is there to help, encourage, and protect.

Christ Dispenses Justice

Perhaps the greatest obstacle to our emotional wholeness is bitterness, the resentment generated when we are mistreated. To see the guilty one go free—the one who ruined our lives—only increases the anger. The injustice of it all causes us to cry out, "Where is God?" The Babylonians mistreated the Israelites when they captured them and took them from Jerusalem to Babylon about the year 586 BC. That was some 2,500 years ago. Our passage, Isaiah 61:1–3, predicts that the Babylonians will fall under the vengeance of God.

That has not yet happened.

Interestingly, when Christ read this passage in the synagogue, He stopped before He reached the phrase "and the day of vengeance of our God" (v. 2). Why? Because vengeance awaits His second coming; it was not to be a part of the first. So, even though the Babylonians were conquered by Cyrus in 539 BC, they still have not yet been fully judged by God. Justice is in the wings, waiting for Christ's return to the Mount of Olives.

If the Israelites have waited for twenty-five centuries and have not yet seen God avenge them, we should not be surprised if we are asked to wait a while for God to "even the score." Someday there will be a resurrection of all individuals who have ever lived. Each personal life will be reviewed in minute detail, day by day, hour by hour. At that time vengeance will be meted out in exact proportion to the sins committed.

What are the implications? If you have been abused, your captor will be brought to trial in heaven even if he should escape trial on earth. Of course, we should do all we can to promote justice, and those who have committed crimes should be dealt with in the courts. However, man can do only so much. There are always loose ends and circumstances where justice has been circumvented. In this life many people escape the judgment due them, but eventually God will rule on every single act that has ever been committed by mortals.

Because forgiveness plays such a great part in the healing of the soul, an entire chapter will be devoted to it later in this book. For now it is sufficient to remember that your abuser has ruined enough of your life; you must, for your own benefit, let go of your anger and entrust your complaint wholly to God.

Should you ever confront your abuser? This should be done only after careful thought and wise counsel. If he or she denies it, a correct response might be, "You may deny it, but God and I both know you are guilty. I now transfer to you all responsibility for what happened." This response can be either verbal or an attitude of the heart, whichever is appropriate to the situation. In either case, having made it, leave it there.

God gives the oppressed dignity by promising they will be vindicated. At last someone will defend them, take up their cause, and stand in their place. What the parents of an abused child did not do, God will accomplish. He will take up the cause of His children, for "the LORD supports the afflicted" (Ps. 147:6 NASB).

What else does Christ do for the brokenhearted?

Christ Comforts Us

You say, "Is there a way to make up for my past?" The years cannot be relived, but God does pour His comfort into our souls. He appoints for us blessings to take away the burdens of the past. Here is what He says He will do for the Israelites.

1. He will give them "a beautiful headdress instead of ashes" (Isa. 61:3).

During times of mourning, the ancients often threw ashes on their heads. God was about to give them a new headpiece.

Does the name *Amnon* mean anything to you? He was one of the sons of David, a half-brother to Absalom. Amnon fell in love with Tamar, who was his half-sister. He wanted to have sexual intercourse with her, so he set a scheme into action. He pretended to be sick and requested that Tamar come into the room to prepare some food for him. When she did this, he jumped up from the bed and asked her to have sex with him. She protested, so in anger he raped her. What do you think that did to the relationship? We read:

> Then Amnon hated her with very great hatred, so that the hatred with which he hated her was greater than the love with which he had loved her. And Amnon said to her, "Get up! Go!" (2 Sam. 13:15)

Tamar had resisted him; now that he was finished with her, he treated her like dirt. Her reply: "No. Sending me away would be even more evil than having raped me." She didn't want to let him get away with this. What did Amnon do? He asked his attendant to throw the woman out and lock the door. For the whole story, read 2 Samuel 13. It details her response to the shame and humiliation.

> Tamar put ashes on her head and tore the long robe that she wore [a symbol of her virginity]. And she laid her hand on her head and went away, crying aloud as she went. (v. 19)

Here was a young woman, raped by an incestuous half-brother, filled with shame and anger. How did she express it? With ashes on her head. Ashes symbolized shame and humiliation.

In the Isaiah passage God says that He will take the ashes away and replace them with a "garland" (Isa. 61:3 NASB), an ornamental headdress used for times of rejoicing. The King James Version translates it "beauty." Yes, the turban was worn for festive occasions and was a symbol of prosperity and victory.

You may have been sexually violated by someone you trusted—a family member, or a friend. Symbolically, you have ashes on your head, but God makes you look beautiful. He affirms the dignity that others have sought to steal from you. And what God thinks matters.

2. He will give them "the oil of gladness instead of mourning" (Isa. 61:3).

Perfumed ointment was poured on guests at joyous feasts. When David wrote, "You anoint my head with oil" (Ps. 23:5), he was speaking of the special treatment God gives those whom He loves. It was a high honor to be anointed with the soothing oil.

If you attended a funeral in ancient times, you did not come with your head anointed with oil. Oil symbolized joy; it was inappropriate in times of grief. God says Israel will be blessed with the oil of gladness. The funeral will give way to the wedding.

God will restore at least some joy if we become His worshipers. We come to Him, not to concentrate on our past, but to give Him the glory He so richly deserves. In His presence our souls are refreshed.

3. He will give them "garment[s] of praise instead of a fainting spirit" (Isa. 61:3).

Your clothing will be bright and beautiful—not the sackcloth that indicates despondency. David wrote:

> I believe that I shall look upon the goodness of the LORD
>> in the land of the living!
> Wait for the LORD;
>> be strong, and let your heart take courage;
>> wait for the LORD!
> (Ps. 27:13–14)

The three blessings God promised the Israelites are outer changes that signify inward healing. The new look without reflects the new joy within. Isaiah concludes:

They may be called oaks of righteousness,
    the planting of the LORD, that he may be glorified.
(Isa. 61:3b)

Just as God liberated the Israelites, so He is ready to help us walk in the light of His love and freedom.

Someone reading this chapter might not be a victim but an abuser. I received an anonymous letter from a man who had abused a boy. He explained the torment he was now going through and said, "I would give anything if I could undo the damage I did to that child."

Yes, abusers are human, too. They do terrible things because they perceive themselves to be locked in their own prison of anger, shame, and perversion. Only God knows the torment of their conscience, the contempt they have for themselves, and the dreadful secrets that hold them bound. Remember, there is no unpardonable sin for those who seek pardon!

STEPS TO FREEDOM

How do you get out from under the burden of your abuser, the person who keeps you in an emotional prison? These steps are not necessarily consecutive; sometimes they are done in reverse order, sometimes simultaneously.

Step #1: Confront Your Past: with Christ

Don't delve into your past alone. You need the help of Christ and also a trusted friend or friends as you share what has happened.

I cannot tell you how much of your past you must relive in order to be emotionally healed. Some find that simply acknowledging the abuses of the past is all that is necessary. Others need to confront their past in more detail. I do not believe that everyone who has been abused needs extensive therapy. Many people spend years sifting through their past only to discover that their investigation has not freed them from its power. Sometimes the more details uncovered, the greater the resentment and anger.

For some people it is enough to know that Jesus Christ is aware of every detail of what happened. There is no rule that fits everyone, but the following guidelines will help.

1. *You do not have to confront all of your past at once.* Take a bit of it—one experience—and relive it in the presence of God, telling Him how you felt, expressing your hurt and anger. Choose to forgive, and give your feelings—yes, your deepest feelings—to God.

2. *You must share your hurt with a trusted friend* or counselor who will feel your pain and share your burden. You must experience the acceptance and love of a human being regardless of what terrible secrets you reveal. Shame, anger, and resentment—your friend must accept all of these outbursts without rejecting you.

3. *Your dignity must be restored by understanding who you are in the presence of God* and in the eyes of others. This will come through the comfort of Christ and His ambassadors, your friend(s).

4. *Some people find help in writing a letter to their abuser,* sharing all their hurt and anger (even if the letter is never sent). Others pretend that the abuser is "sitting" in an empty chair, and they speak what is on their mind to that chair. These methods may be helpful in getting your past and its hurts out into the open.

You will need courage to embark on this journey. Let me assure you of one fact: There is nothing you will uncover in your past that you and God cannot handle.

Step #2: Commit Your Past: to Christ

You may find there are many loose ends you can never resolve on earth. Your abuser may be dead; or he may be living somewhere, totally unconcerned about the wounds he inflicted on you. When he greets you, he may act as if nothing happened. You have only one recourse if you are to be emotionally whole; you must turn all of these matters over to God—you must completely separate yourself from the burden of seeing these matters resolved on earth. Some people can do this more easily than others, but it must be done.

Your trust in God will grow. Because God did not defend or avenge you when you were abused, you may say, "I can never trust Him." But trust Him you must. Both your past and your future must be left in His hands. Victims of abuse can never make peace with their cruel earthly father until they have made peace with their loving heavenly Father.

If you ask why God did not intervene when you were abused, I cannot answer. What if He wanted to demonstrate that He can make someone emotionally whole despite his or her past? What if He wanted to prove that some people will continue to love Him whether He rescues them from their tormentors or not? These matters are hidden in His secret counsels. He is the God who wounds, but He also heals (Deut. 32:39). The fact that He loves you and cares for you is clear in Scripture. The whys and wherefores are less so. Confidence in God is absolutely essential to emotional growth.

Step #3: Close Your Past: with Christ

Over time, the power of past memories will diminish. With time it will not be necessary to recall all of the details. Again, you must remember that loving God is more important than your own well-being. Emotional healing is often a by-product of a single-minded commitment to seek God. Would you be willing to endure your pain if because of it you came to know God better?

If you broke your arm, God could heal it instantly. It is more likely, however, that it would take several weeks or months. Healing a broken heart is also a process, not an event. For many the open wound becomes a scar—healing is taking place.

God can turn victims into survivors.

He heals the brokenhearted
and binds up their wounds.
(Ps. 147:3)

For my father and my mother have forsaken me,
but the LORD will take me in.
(Ps. 27:10)

ACTION STEP

Mentally walk through the steps mentioned above. Memorize Romans 8:18 and 2 Corinthians 4:16–18. As you share your past with a counselor, let your future hope motivate you to present faithfulness. Remember, you will be rewarded if you suffer well.

Chapter 6

Understanding Sexual Bonds

I hate him for what he did to me, but I'd marry him today if he asked me to!"

This eighteen-year-old girl had every right to loathe her pseudo-lover, a married man who had awakened her sexuality by his advances and seductions. He promised that she would be his sweetheart forever, so she felt secure in his affection. But when the affair was discovered, he blamed everything on her, falsely accusing her of initiating this sexual liaison. She was betrayed and humiliated and was asked to leave the church they both attended.

Yet, incredibly, she was willing to risk everything and marry him if only he would ask! Despite the fact that he was married and the father of three children, this young Christian woman was willing to break up a marriage to have the affection of this man, the first with whom she had had a sexual relationship.

This experience was so indelibly stamped on her soul that even the man's betrayal could not chisel him out of her heart. When she realized that he would not leave his wife and children for her, she sought fulfillment with other lovers, going from one man to another to satisfy her awakened longings for intimacy. Even if she didn't particularly enjoy these liaisons, she felt, in her words, "this is the price I have to pay to mean something to somebody."

A few of the questions these chapters attempt to answer are: Why is the first sexual experience so important in forming our attitudes toward sexuality? And why can one immoral relationship begin a search for other sexual partners in a vain attempt to find fulfillment? What are the steps needed to bring emotional and spiritual healing to those who are sexually broken?

Our sexuality is the most sensitive aspect of our personality. We are fundamentally sexual beings with deep inner needs that we are tempted to satisfy even at great risk. If we do not channel these desires correctly, we can embark on a destructive path filled with broken promises that will eventually lead us to a painful dead end.

Pornography is not the only doorway to the world of sexual brokenness, but it is one of the most popular. Young people who watch movies replete with various forms of sexuality find their passions so stimulated that they want to act out everything they have seen. Any thought that disease or an STD might frighten them into maintaining their virginity till marriage seems ill-founded. Given the fact that those who have sex before marriage jeopardize their chances for a happy relationship (the reasons will be explained later), it is understandable that we have so many sexual problems in marriages.

Then there are those who commit adultery, or drift into the world of sexual aberrations. Sadomasochism, cross-dressing, and homosexuality increase as those driven by sexual desires join the frantic quest to find fulfillment with the right partner. Others are victims, suffering from the sexual aggression of predators. As we have already seen, it is estimated that one in five girls born this year will be sexually molested by a relative, neighbor, or trusted friend. Early in my ministry I would speak about the fulfillment and joy of sex. Now, after a few more years of listening to marriage problems, I realize that for many people sex is not a positive experience. Some women who were molested as children find sex to be a difficult, if not a revolting, experience. At least a few have been raped; others were talked into early sexual experiences that have had a devastating effect on their current relationships.

Sex can either become a source of maximum fulfillment or maximum grief. A biblical understanding of sexuality will answer many questions about the power of sexual experiences and, more important, tell how to break the power of those relationships. Above all, there is hope; God can help people move from sexual slavery to sexual sanity.

Please commit yourself to this reading. Only when we understand the whys and wherefores of sexuality will we be able to appreciate the healing that Christ offers to all who come to Him in honest confession.

SEXUALITY AND CREATION

Think of it. Although Adam had the awesome privilege of walking with God in the Garden of Eden, the Lord said that something important was still missing! "It is not good that the man should be alone; I will make him a helper fit for him" (Gen. 2:18). God unmistakably affirms that man is a social creature and needs companionship that is "fit" for him.

When God created Adam, He chose to use the dust of the ground for the raw material. "Then the LORD God formed the man of dust from the ground and breathed into his nostrils the breath of life, and the man became a living creature" (Gen. 2:7).

We might expect that God would shape a similar form from dust when He created Eve. But we read, "So the LORD God caused a deep sleep to fall upon the man, and while he slept took one of his ribs and closed up its place with flesh. And the rib that the LORD God had taken from the man he made into a woman and brought her to the man" (Gen. 2:21–22).

In the creation account, God pronounces that it is not good for the man to be alone, and He creates a helper for him; so it was our Creator's intention from the beginning that we desire each other. Eve was taken out of Adam's flesh, signifying the unity God would bring about when they are reunited in marriage. God gave Adam and Eve different characteristics; likewise, once they had rebelled in the garden, both would receive unique judgments for the sin they had committed, and conflict would be introduced into their relationship. Both men and women were created in the image of God, though they reflect God in different ways. And yet, their desire for one another would be strong and a new bond between them would be formed in marriage. And so, both sexes created in the image of God, yet spiritually fallen, would be brought together in marriage to represent a concrete display of the relationship between Christ and the church.

In the creation account we see the roots of our sexual desire, proof that sex was created by God as an expression of unity and love between a man and a woman. Our sexual identity cannot be ignored or misused without serious consequences. Several implications follow.

Sexual Desire Is God-Ordained

First, we must accept our sexual desires as from God. The desire for sexual intimacy is a yearning for completeness. There is a magnetic attraction between a man and a woman that is innate, powerful, and unyielding.

God's entire plan for the human race was dependent on the sex drive inherent within every human being. If Adam had not been sexually attracted to Eve, the human race would have ended with the death of our two parents. But God made the desire for physical intimacy so strong that there was no chance Adam would look at Eve and walk away!

We can become sexually stimulated without any conscious decision on our part. The presence of an attractive member of the opposite sex, or the fantasies of love that play in our minds, or just the activity of our sex glands without any external stimulation—all of these trigger desires for intimacy and sexual expression.

Of course, we are responsible for what we do with these involuntary sexual feelings. Both the Old Testament and the New give specific instruction on what sexual activity is permissible and what is not. Christ taught that when a man lusts for (that is, sexually covets) a woman who is not his, he has already committed adultery in his heart. We are created with powerful natural forces of attraction that must be controlled.

This doesn't mean that it is God's will for everyone to marry. Some may desire marriage but have not found a suitable partner. Others may have the gift of celibacy, as evidently Paul had (1 Cor. 7:7). Of course, singles are also created in the image of God, though they may represent Him in a different way, and singleness might actually be of special benefit to those who serve the Lord (1 Cor. 7:32–36).

Though the sex drive is powerful, no person need think that sex is necessary for either happiness or fulfillment. Many who are single testify to the contentment of their lifestyle. Others who are married may not be able to have sex because of physical disabilities or other mitigating factors.

It is not necessary to have sex in order to accept our sexuality. Masculinity and femininity have their individual characteristics, drives, and aspirations. These must be accepted, whether one is married or single.

We Must Positively Affirm Our Own Sexuality

Second, our sexuality must be positively affirmed. Most of us were brought up with some very necessary warnings about illicit sexual expression. But if this is all that we know about what God says on the subject, we will live with a sense of shame, or at least embarrassment. The prohibitions of Scripture, such as "Thou shalt not commit adultery," are only one side of the coin; the other is to understand God's intention in giving us these desires. We must strive to govern our sexuality in such a way that it will fulfill us and not destroy us.

Many Christian adolescents wanting to live a pure moral life think that all sexual desires are shameful. They forget that to feel a powerful attraction to some member of the opposite sex is precisely what God intended. The very act of thanking God for such desires reminds us that our feelings are not a cause for shame but joy. Our battle against lust actually increases when sexuality is viewed as "dirty." When we accept the fact that these desires in themselves were pronounced good by God, we can be free to rejoice and more earnestly desire to use them according to God's specifications.

To the ancient Jews, sex within marriage was properly considered as a holy act. On his wedding night it was believed that a man actually went into the Holy of Holies when he made love to his wife. Let us not call unclean what God has called holy. Let us celebrate our sexuality, rejoicing in God's creation. This will help us view our masculinity and femininity from God's perspective.

SEXUALITY AND MARRIAGE

What is marriage? In marriage a man and a woman are joined by two bonds. The first is a covenant, an agreement that they will live together until "death does them part." The sex act creates the second bond that joins them, body, soul, and spirit.

Some Bible scholars teach that since sex bonds two people together, couples who have shared a bed are already married. According to this view, premarital sex does not exist, for sex equals marriage. This teaching has caused young people to get married, even to a partner they neither loved nor respected. Their reasoning was clear: If they were already married in the sight of God, they should complete the union by having a formal wedding ceremony. However, I do not believe that sexual intercourse of itself constitutes marriage. A man and woman are made husband and wife by a covenant taken in the presence of God and witnesses. The Lord rebuked Israelite men for mistreating their wives and said to each of the men, "She is your companion and your wife by covenant" (Mal. 2:14). The covenant justifies the sexual relationship; the sexual relationship does not justify the covenant.

It is true that the Bible does not describe the wedding ceremony as we know it. But the bride and groom did enter into an agreement, even if it was not ratified in the same way as it is today. Even in the case of Isaac and Rebekah, a covenant was made between Abraham (Isaac's father) and Laban and Bethuel (Rebekah's brother and father). This agreement was spoken by Abraham's servant (Gen. 24:48–49). Gifts were given to signify the betrothal.

As cultures change, so do the customs accompanying the wedding ceremony. But one thing is certain: A couple should not live together without the benefit of a solemn covenantal agreement. Sex binds two people together emotionally and spiritually, but the covenant comes first, establishing the permanent bond.

Today millions of couples are living together without the benefit of a marriage covenant. In most instances this arrangement serves as a back door of escape, just in case the relationship does not work out. But this arrangement communicates a confusing dual message. On the one hand the partners are saying to each other, "I love you so much I want to be sexually intimate with you." On the other hand, the second message is, "I don't want to get too close to you, so I have the option of escaping in case you don't meet all of my needs." According to P. Roger Hillerstrom, "the result of this double message is an inbred lack of confidence in the relationship."[21] Understandably, these seeds of doubt bear bitter fruit later on.

To those who ask, "What difference does a piece of paper make?" another question should be asked: "Would you purchase a house without a formal agreement?" One reason for the formal agreement is to close the door to any possibility that one of the parties will back out when a better deal comes along. Marriage, of course, is much more important than purchasing a house. There can be no security in the relationship without a formal covenant to secure the relationship.

To carry the analogy of purchasing a house one step further, after the papers are signed, you have the right to move into the new premises and enjoy them. After the marriage covenant, the couple now has the right to enjoy one another in the sexual relationship.

After the covenant, comes the sexual bonding. Some think of this only as a physical bond; but if it were, sex would only be a biological experience (as the humanists affirm). But sex is much more than a physical experience; it actually bonds two persons—body, soul, and spirit. One person who bears the image of God stamps his or her personality upon the partner who also bears the image of God.

Marriage reflects the plurality and unity of the Godhead. Though God exists in three persons, we read, "Hear, O Israel: The LORD our God, the LORD is one" (Deut. 6:4). The same Hebrew word for "one" (*ehad*) is used for the marriage union: "They shall become one flesh" (Gen. 2:24). Just as it is unthinkable that members of the Trinity would operate as separate entities, so a husband and wife should operate together—diversity within unity. The bond that has been formed involves the total personality of each partner; it is a unity with plurality.

Sex creates a "soul-tie" between two people, forming the most intimate of all human relationships. When the Bible says, "Adam knew Eve his wife" (Gen. 4:1 KJV), the word *know* is not simply a euphemism for the sex act. Sexual intercourse actually consummates the highest form of human interpersonal communication and knowledge. Indeed, this exclusive familiarity cannot be easily erased. Once a man and a woman have had sex together, nothing can be the same between them ever again. There simply is no such thing as a brand-new beginning.

God intended that the first experience be enjoyed by a man and a woman who are wholly committed to each other within the protection of a covenant. That was to assure the acceptance and unconditional love that guard the most intimate of all human relationships.

Once this bond has been established, it must be nurtured, strengthened, and kept pure. This happens through mutual caring, the development of trust and respect. When the commitment is threatened, the sexual fulfillment (at least on the part of one partner, if not both) is diminished.

SEXUALITY AND ALIEN BONDS

Unfortunately, our world is filled with people who have experienced alien, or sinful, bonds. That is, they have been bonded sexually without a covenant of marriage.

Perhaps one of the most surprising passages in the New Testament regarding the nature of sexuality is found in Paul's words to the church in Corinth:

> Do you not know that your bodies are members of Christ? Shall I then take the members of Christ and make them members of a prostitute? Never! Or do you not know that he who is joined to a prostitute becomes one body with her? For, as it is written, "The two will become one flesh." (1 Cor. 6:15–16)

We would all agree that sex with a prostitute is sex without a commitment, sex without any hint of mutual respect or caring. Prostitution is based on raw lust, sex for mutual exploitation. Yet, incredibly, Paul says that God joins the prostitute to her partner and "the two will become one flesh." To prove it he quotes from Genesis 2:24, where in Eden God joined Adam and Eve into one. Sex of any kind always bonds people together, body, soul, and spirit.

Such bonds are outside the boundaries and nurture of a marriage covenant. These bonds intrude, violating what God intended. Two persons have come together in an intimate union without the security of a covenant based on respect and trust.

A woman whose husband asked forgiveness for his promiscuity said, "I feel as if all the other women he has had sex with are in bed there with me." In a sense she was right. AIDS researchers tell us that when we have a sexual relationship, we are, in effect, having sex with all the people with whom our partner has had sex. This is true medically, but it is also true metaphysically. Because sex joins people into one flesh, past bonds are still there.

The Power of the First Bond

What are some of the consequences of alien bonds? First, we must recognize the power of the first bond. The first sexual experience or experiences are so powerful that they can even determine the direction of a person's sexual orientation. A boy recruited by an older gay man may initially hate the experience, but because sex bonds two people together, he may begin to feel a sense of security and fulfillment within this relationship. Soon he seeks out other partners, not because he was born gay but because his initial experiences were so stamped upon his soul that he follows the lead of his newly awakened desires.

This also explains why a young woman may marry a man with whom she has slept, even though he may be abusive. His personality is so indelibly imprinted on her mind and heart that she feels an obligation to become his wife. Also, because of sex he may have incredible power over her. He can mistreat her, but she will always return to him. Even if the relationship ends, it is difficult for her to put him out of her mind.

Given the importance of the first sexual experience, we should not be surprised that some married partners are tempted to return to a previous sexual partner, often the first one with whom they had a relationship. Recently I received a letter from a woman who heard a message I gave at a couples conference. Despite the fact that she was happily married, she had sought out a former boyfriend, her first sexual lover. The power of a previous relationship was still there.

Young people should take note: One reason they should guard their virginity is that after they have been sexually bonded, nothing can ever be the same again. That special sexual experience is best enjoyed within the security and trust of a covenant.

The Road to Promiscuity

Second, alien bonds often lead to promiscuity. Once a sexual bond has been formed, there will be a desire to maintain that bond or seek other ones to replace it. Therefore, one sexual experience outside of marriage can begin a spiral of illicit relationships. Once a person has crossed a forbidden sexual barrier, he or she might have a powerful desire to do so again and again.

A young woman who was a virgin had a sexual encounter with her boyfriend in a moment of passion. After the romantic relationship ended (as they usually do), both of them independently sought a whole series of sexual encounters with different partners. When the girl got pregnant, she had no idea who the father might be.

The first bond created a "soul-tie" that could not be easily dismissed. After the initial experience, nothing could ever quite be the same. Now that this woman could no longer maintain the bond with the first mate, she sought others to find the fulfillment she craved. A thirst for intimacy had developed that she tried to satisfy. Since she felt defiled, there seemed to be no reason to forgo her sexual quest.

A man discovered on his wedding night that his wife was not a virgin. He became so angry that he vowed to "even the score." On their honeymoon he took a walk down the street and found a prostitute. Five years later he admitted that that one act had led to an addiction that he had secretly nurtured three or four times a week. The power of one alien bond!

Today much is written about sexual addiction, but such slavery has existed from the beginning of time. Those who begin the pattern of alien bonding tend to continue it, seeking a fulfillment which, of necessity, must elude them. One writer said of sexual addicts, "They use sex like a drug, not to consummate loving relationships but rather to drown the pain of feeling empty inside a dark, shameful well of sexual oblivion."[22]

Individuals seldom have an abiding commitment to alien bonds. And because they have experienced intimacy outside the proper boundaries, they will now have a tendency to forgo any process of courtship and almost immediately seek genital intimacy. Now that the principle of a covenant relationship has been violated, the temptation to continue the pattern will be persistent and powerful.

Many people are seeking love and acceptance through the sexual relationship, but, of course, they do not find it there. A girl who did not have a warm relationship with her father may be tempted to seek love in the arms of other men. She is convinced that given enough time she will find the ultimate partner. Each time she says, "This will be different," but in the end it turns out to be the same failed relationship. The greater her guilt and emptiness, the more she will be driven to continue her hopeless search. She is looking for true love and acceptance in all the wrong places.

True, there are times when an alien bond does not immediately lead to promiscuity. Some adulterers have been known to be faithful to their illicit partner. But remember that such a person has already violated his covenant with his spouse; therefore, to violate his commitment to his illicit lover will not be difficult when the right time comes.

This explains why a man who commits immorality may lapse even after he has confessed his sin and turned to others for counsel. Sexual addicts, like alcoholics, tend to repeat their behavior patterns even after the sincerest attempt at reform. As we shall see, this cycle can indeed be broken, but the temptation will always be there.

Those who know how to repent and come under the authority of one of God's representatives will find strength to form wholesome relationships; such a person can stop the strong impulse to repeat the same sin. Battles must be won, one day at a time.

The Elusive Exclusive Bond

Third, alien bonds often make it difficult to create an exclusive bond. Incredibly, I've heard some couples talk as if premarital relations are acceptable, but that after marriage the couple must practice sexual faithfulness. In actuality, the marriage ceremony does not change an individual. Some who have been promiscuous will fear an exclusive bond, unsure whether they can be true to such a commitment. Others who try to focus on one relationship find that their marriage partner cannot fill the emptiness that past relationships generated in their lives. Memories can be so powerful that no present relationship can compare with the titillation of past illicit affairs.

Those who come to marriage with a multitude of sexual relationships will never form a strong new bond until the power of the previous ones have been broken. Time itself does not heal all wounds; the past must be confronted in the presence of God.

Finally, there is guilt, the restless conscience that leads to anger and depression. Many people deny that they feel guilty about their liaisons, but they cannot escape the consequences built into God's moral law. He did not create us for alien bonds; they violate His will. Sexuality is such a sensitive part of who we are as persons. There will always be a residue of guilt that surfaces in these relationships, plaguing the conscience, quickening past memories, and stifling true joy.

Eventually, the guilt turns to shame. Whereas guilt tells us we have *done* wrong, shame says we *are* wrong. These feelings can bind people in self-hatred and condemnation. Often the roots of such feelings develop within a dysfunctional family and are magnified through sexual misconduct.

Little wonder so many marriages are in difficulty. Young people may say to themselves, "Let's have this sexual relationship, then we will ask God to forgive us, and we will start all over again—everything will be just as it was before. After all, if God can't forgive us for this, what is the blood of Christ for?" Yes, the blood of Christ does forgive, but the power of the past sexual experience will still be there.

Thankfully, God is able to enter into the picture and bring both cleansing and sexual wholeness. He is the only one qualified to give us the rules by which we are to live, and He is also qualified to pick us up out of the moral quagmire.

How can these bonds be broken? And what can be done in the lives of those who are even now plagued with past memories? These issues will be explored in the next chapter.

ACTION STEP

Think of ways to "flee from temptation." You might have to relocate to get away from a person or situation that is causing you to fall into sin. Perhaps you should unsubscribe from a streaming service, block access to inappropriate websites, or avoid going out alone at night.

Keep close accounts with the person to whom you are accountable. The pain of honesty is better than the pain of secrecy.

Chapter 7

Breaking Sexual Bonds

A Christian man who had a responsible position in a Christian school began an affair with a woman he met at church. Though his wife suspected his unfaithfulness, he denied it, even asserting, "If I am lying, let God strike me dead!"

Because God did not take him up on his heroic challenge, he felt comfortable in continuing the relationship. When he was unable to deny it any longer, he wept in repentance, asking forgiveness of both his wife and God. And yet despite his sincere attempts at reconciliation, he secretly continued the relationship, eventually leaving his wife for his new partner. To quote his words exactly, "I know I'm doing wrong, but I am helpless to do otherwise. I am driven to be with her, no matter the cost."

The easy explanation is to say that the man was not truly repentant. But once again, we must remember that alien bonds often give partners incredible power over one another. All rational considerations for his wife and children were tossed to the wind; all that he cared for was being with her. Never mind that after he got a divorce and married his adulterous lover, their new marriage ended in disaster.

In crossing the barrier into the forbidden world of illicit love, he was trapped by a power greater than his own strength. Little wonder the author of Proverbs warns a young man about prostitution and pessimistically predicts, "For her house sinks down to death, and her paths to the departed; none who go to her come back, nor do they regain the paths of life" (Prov. 2:18–19).

Thankfully, there is another side to the story. With God's help, a man or woman can come back from a life of immorality. There is hope on almost every page of the Bible.

To illustrate Christ's power, we will look at the story of a woman who was guilty of numerous illicit bonds but was brought to emotional and spiritual wholeness. Women are more sensitive and often feel the pain of immorality more deeply than men. The fact that she was given a new identity and inner peace should be an encouragement to all who are haunted by a sexual past.

Her story is recorded in Luke 7:36–50.

Simon was a Pharisee who threw a feast for Christ because he wanted to check out this miracle worker for himself. In those days, uninvited guests were welcome to attend as long as they sat along the wall of the room and did not expect to be seated at the table. Evidently, this feast was well-publicized, and perhaps a number of uninvited guests came. Among these was a woman who is described as "a sinner."

Since all people are sinners, it is clear that Luke wants us to understand that this woman was a sinner of a special sort, namely, an immoral woman. Almost certainly she was a prostitute, a woman who was known to have many alien bonds.

Those of us who are interested in the causes of human behavior would find it interesting to know how she fell into such a lifestyle. Perhaps she was brought up in a good home but chose a path of rebellion. One relationship led to another until she decided to sell her body to make some money from her immorality. Also possible is the likelihood that she was sexually abused when growing up and this led to an insatiable appetite for love and affection, so she turned to men for attention. Or maybe she was betrayed by her husband, became angry, and decided to take out her hostility against God and men by turning to prostitution. The men she hated could be used to earn a living, exacting as much payment as the market could bear.

Whatever the scenario, here was a woman whose memories were flooded with the stain of illicit relationships. When she heard that Jesus was to be in the house of Simon, she decided to be there at all costs.

The visitors were seated at a low table, perhaps a foot higher than the floor. In those days they would recline at such a table, each person leaning toward his left, propped up by his left arm, and free to eat with his right hand. This woman, seeing Christ reclining at the table, went behind Him and took her vial of precious perfume and began to pour its contents on His extended feet. As she did this, tears poured down her cheeks and in a moment Christ's feet were drenched. Then she wiped His feet with her hair. This act of devotion was done repeatedly, unashamedly.

This was too much for Simon. He was embarrassed, even if Christ wasn't. He said to himself, "If this man were a prophet, he would have known who and what sort of woman this is who is touching him, for she is a sinner" (7:39).

What an incredible story! Here is this woman in the presence of both Christ and a Pharisee. Yet here she found emotional wholeness. In the end, the Lord of Glory told her, "Go in peace" (v. 50). What more could an immoral woman ask?

A HEART WILLING TO BREAK WITH THE PAST

In the presence of Christ this woman, awash with shame, experienced God's cleansing. She heard Christ say, "Your faith has saved you; go in peace" (v. 50). She did in a few moments what it takes some people months to do. She was ready to put her past behind her.

Notice her attitude.

Honesty

This woman had no time for hypocrisy or pretense. She had the reputation of being a sinner and evidently deserved it. She knew that coming to the house of a self-righteous Pharisee would elicit derision and scorn. To her, this did not matter because she overcame her natural inclination to hide in her shame. *Her desire to meet Christ was more powerful than her desire to avoid public scorn.* The insults she experienced on the streets were nothing in comparison to the moral derision she would get from this arrogant bigot and his friends. Yet, there she was.

Many people with her history find neither power over their past nor strength for their future. One reason is that their shame is stronger than their desire for honesty. Sex addicts or those with a sordid sexual past often develop layers of denial, virtually insulating themselves from who they really are and what they have done. This is part of the reason why the adulterer referred to at the beginning of the chapter was unable to break his relationship.

The grace of God does not enter closed doors but works only when deception gives way to honest exposure and humble admission of sin. Most people caught in sexual sin deny it, only admitting to what has been uncovered. This desire to hide allows the root of sin to remain intact.

The first step toward breaking the power of an immoral past is, in the words of another, "to die to the natural inclination to live a lie." God will do miracles for those who are so weary of their sinful secrets that they are prepared to "come clean" before God and all whom they have wronged.

An honest admission of one's past is also necessary for those who are victims of other people's sins or crimes. Those who were molested as children, those who have been raped or otherwise abused must be willing to face their past in the presence of Christ. Other qualified believers must also be a part of the healing process. Do not think you must change to make yourself worthy of coming to Christ. Simply come as you are, openly, honestly, expectantly. "Whoever conceals his transgressions will not prosper, but he who confesses and forsakes them will obtain mercy" (Prov. 28:13).

Faith

Second, she had faith. Christ said of her, "Your faith has saved you; go in peace" (Luke 7:50). Her tears did not save her, nor the loving act of pouring expensive perfume on Christ's feet. Her good deeds did not bring the salvation of God to her soul. Faith, and faith alone, in Christ's forgiveness and salvation wiped her sins away.

But her kindness was evidence of her faith. She believed that Christ would accept her despite the fact that He knew all about her past. Perhaps it was the kindness in Christ's face, or maybe she had listened to His messages of love and hope. Whatever the case, there in the presence of Christ her faith blossomed; she knew that this man would not use and then discard her as so many others had.

How thankful she was that Christ was not a Pharisee! Imagine what would have happened if He had said to her, "Woman, I don't appreciate being touched by a prostitute—don't you know that I am the Holy Son of God? Go back to the streets where you belong!" If she had been rejected by the only One qualified to forgive her, there was no other place in the universe where she might go to be forgiven. If the Son of God should turn His back, there was but eternal despair. But if He should speak a word of forgiveness, there was eternal joy!

A young woman wrote to me saying that an older woman had convinced her that they should have a sexual relationship. Although initially resistant, she gave in, and thus began a five-year struggle with lesbianism. "Oh, how I stink in the core of my being!" she writes, "I know God has forgiven me, but I cannot forgive myself. Many times I cannot help but cry. I feel so tired and old. Is there any hope for someone like me? God forbid that I should be a Judas, who felt sorry for what he had done but nevertheless chose to go in the wrong direction!"

Yes! A thousand times yes, there is hope.

But why does she still feel defiled though she has confessed her sins, perhaps many times? First, she must not only claim God's forgiveness but also His cleansing, which is her right. Her conscience can be wiped clean; she can live without the voices of condemnation and the heaviness that comes with a defiled conscience.

Second, as mentioned in an earlier chapter, she may be making the error of confusing the accusations of the devil with the voice of the Holy Spirit. The responsibility of the Holy Spirit is to convict us of sin so that we might confess it; after that, the work of the Spirit to convict ends. But at this point Satan usually takes over and tries to imitate the work of God and convict us of sins that God has already forgiven! Believers who think the accusations of the devil are the convictions of the Spirit are caught in a vicious cycle of continual confession without the assurance of forgiveness. Or they believe the lie that they must live with guilt as a payment for sin.

Forgiveness and cleansing are available for *all* sins. "If we confess our sins, he is faithful and just to forgive us our sins and to cleanse us from all unrighteousness" (1 John 1:9).

When Christ died on the cross, His death was a payment for the sins of immorality committed by His children. Why should anyone think that he or she must pay a second time? If you have confessed your sin, the next time Satan reminds you of your past, remind him of his future!

If a prostitute can believe in the presence of Christ two thousand years ago, a lesbian can believe today. Both can hear the voice of the Savior, "Your faith has saved you; go in peace."

Facing the Pain

She wept; she wept profusely. Her tears ran down her cheeks and fell onto Christ's feet. The present tense of the verbs indicates that she *kept on* weeping, *kept on* anointing His feet, *kept on* wiping His feet with her hair. Her tears proved that she was willing to face her pain; she faced the hurts buried in her sordid past.

Why did she weep? We cannot know, but we can surmise the reasons. First, think of the men who had betrayed her! The broken promises, the assurances of protection and love. Then after they used her, she was tossed aside like the peelings of an orange. She was stripped of her sense of value and self-worth.

She may also have wept because of the grief of broken relationships. Perhaps she met a married man whom she dearly loved, yet knew that this friendship would have to be permanently broken. Those who are in alien bonds must understand that breaking such relationships sometimes involves the same emotional loss as the death of a spouse. Perhaps she was in mourning.

Another reason she may have been weeping was that she remembered a family that had been broken by her own sin. She may have remembered a sexual relationship with a man whose marriage was ruined because of her relationship with him. Children were deprived of the security of a happy father and mother, and she was an accomplice in it all. Weep she might!

She could have taken all of these feelings and stuffed them deep within her soul, unwilling to face the pain of the past. Then she would have become a tough woman, defiant and angry. She could have told herself, *I will handle my pain and manage my life quite well on my own. I will not let my feelings get to me, no matter the cost!*

Or she could have simply pursued continuous compulsive relationships to deaden the pain of an empty life. She could have continued to flit from one relationship to another, unwilling to admit the fruitlessness of her search for meaning.

Almost every person struggling with a history of sexual broken-ness has a moment of truth, a time when he or she is finally willing to confront the pain that has been pushed down in the depths of the soul. For every alien bond there is at least one hurting heart.

I do not mean to imply that we cannot be forgiven unless we weep; nor do I want to imply that her tears paid for her misdeeds. But sexual sin almost always involves deep pain that is pushed to the bottom of the soul. God has given us tear ducts as a release for our hurt. Through a willingness to confront our pain we are slowly healed.

Those who have been abused must also be willing to weep. It is said that children who have been abused have "no place in the depths of their soul where they may cry their eyes out." Whether you suffer from sins done against you or sins you have committed, there is pain in the depths of your soul. If it has never been confronted, weep in the presence of Christ. Tears are not only permissible but welcome.

Accepting Christ's Forgiveness

Fourth, the prostitute accepted Christ's affirmation of forgiveness. Christ used the occasion to give Simon a lesson in forgiveness.

"A certain moneylender had two debtors. One owed five hundred denarii, and the other fifty. When they could not pay, he cancelled the debt of both. Now which of them will love him more?" Simon answered, "The one, I suppose, for whom he cancelled the larger debt." And he said to him, "You have judged rightly." (Luke 7:41–43)

Then Christ made His point. He reminded Simon,

"Do you see this woman? I entered your house; you gave me no water for my feet, but she has wet my feet with her tears and wiped them with her hair. You gave me no kiss, but from the time I came in she has not ceased to kiss my feet.

You did not anoint my head with oil, but she has anointed my feet with ointment. Therefore I tell you, her sins, which are many, are forgiven—for she loved much. But he who is forgiven little, loves little." (vv. 44–47)

Christ taught that the degree of our love depends on the degree of our forgiveness. Of course, this should not be interpreted to mean that Simon could never love Christ deeply because he had but few sins that needed forgiveness. Christ's intent was to teach that those who *think* they need little forgiveness love only little. Those who see their sin with clearer eyes will love much.

Obviously, this woman did not need forgiveness more than Simon! She saw her sin and this Pharisee saw her sin, but he could not see his own! His self-righteousness stood in the way of his forgiveness. As a result, he was also unable to love.

But to this woman who in humility saw herself for what she was, Christ said, "Your sins are forgiven" (v. 48).

Right in the presence of this self-righteousness, Christ declares this woman forgiven! Perhaps for the first time in years someone actually spoke to her in kindness; someone gave her the dignity of letting those around her know that she was special to God. What blessed words, "You are forgiven!"

I have counseled many people who committed sexual sins and simply could not receive God's forgiveness. Again, we must encourage those who don't feel worthy to be forgiven. Of course, no one deserves it! Forgiveness is a free gift based upon the merit of Christ. That's why God does not find it more difficult to forgive big sins than He does small ones!

Let me say with clarity: *It is God's will that you be totally cleared of the guilt of your sin regardless of the awful consequences it produced.* If David could be forgiven for adultery and killing Uriah, why cannot others be forgiven of a sexual sin despite its consequences?

If this sounds like a misuse of grace, keep in mind that such cleansing involves submission; it implies a willingness to do whatever is necessary to be fully right with God and man.

As for those who cannot forgive themselves: If the supreme lawgiver of the universe has pronounced you clean, do you have the right to pronounce yourself dirty? "Who shall bring any charge against God's elect? It is God who justifies. Who is to condemn? Christ Jesus is the one who died—more than that, who was raised— who is at the right hand of God, who indeed is interceding for us" (Rom. 8:33–34).

Christ is not physically present on earth to tell us, *Your sins are forgiven,* but through His Word we can say exactly those words to those who have confessed their sins. Sometimes I personally have given people that assurance on the basis of Scripture.

Must you live with remorse? No, for remorse is simply repentance made out of sight of Christ. Standing before Him, the conscience is cleansed, and the guilt is transferred to the crucified Christ.

Praise God for His forgiveness regardless of your past! Accept a clear conscience and the cleansing that is your right as a child of God. Rather than repeatedly confessing your sin, affirm the fact that you have been forgiven (Ps. 32:1–2).

Broken Bonds

Christ's final words to this woman were, "Go in peace" (Luke 7:50). In another account, we read that the Pharisees brought a woman to Christ who was caught in adultery. They asked Christ what to do with her, reminding Him that the law commanded such should be stoned. He agreed that they could go ahead and stone her, except that the person who was without sin among them (that is, the person who is free of the same sin they accused her of) should be the first to cast a stone. They all, pierced by their own consciences, walked away, leaving only Christ and the woman. Christ's response: "Neither do I condemn you; go, and from now on sin no more" (John 8:11).

Go—*and sin no more!* Break those sinful relationships that keep causing you to sin! Now that you have come to Christ and received His forgiveness, you must take the next steps to lay your past to rest.

MAKING A DECISION THAT LASTS

In the next chapter forgiveness will be discussed in detail, but here I want to introduce some of its aspects.

Forgive Others

Let me remind you that if you have been wronged, you must choose to forgive all who have mistreated you. This may take time, but it must be done by an act of the will and with the power of God. Resist any tendency to retain your anger because you crave justice. Your desire for justice is legitimate, but you must wholly give your complaint to God. "Beloved, never avenge yourselves, but leave it to the wrath of God, for it is written, 'Vengeance is mine, I will repay,' says the Lord" (Rom. 12:19).

Christ, when speaking of adultery and lust, said, "If your right eye causes you to sin, tear it out and throw it away. For it is better that you lose one of your members than that your whole body be thrown into hell" (Matt. 5:29). He says simply, *Do anything you have to do so that you will not keep sliding into the pit of sexual sin.* That includes forgiving those who have wronged us and becoming accountable to those who can help us stand against past behavioral patterns.

Believe God's Word

Second, believe the Word of God and not your conscience, memory, or emotions. If you are a believer, you are in Christ, seated above all principalities and powers. You are not an adulterer, a homosexual, or a rejected child. You are a child of the King, with all rights and privileges pertaining to such honor. Memorize Scripture that speaks of your position in Christ. "And because of him you are in Christ Jesus, who became to us wisdom from God, righteousness and sanctification and redemption" (1 Cor. 1:30).

Appropriate the Power of the Holy Spirit

Third, accept the power of the Holy Spirit, who is given to believers. Through faith receive His strength, which is given to bring emotional wholeness to any needy heart. The destructive memories of the past must be replaced by "love, joy, peace, patience, kindness, goodness, faithfulness, gentleness, [and] self-control" (Gal. 5:22–23).

Fight the Good Fight

We must learn to resist Satan and enlist others who will pray against his power. Remember, *we will always be tempted to return to the sin that once was our master.*

In chapter 1 we learned that forgiveness and reconciliation exist for those in Christ. When Hosea's wife drifted from one lover to another, he said that one day he would win her back and she would sing again, as in the days of her youth. Then Hosea adds, speaking of the Lord directly but also of himself, "I will betroth you to me forever. I will betroth you to me in righteousness and in justice, in steadfast love and in mercy. I will betroth you to me in faithfulness. And you shall know the LORD" (Hos. 2:19–20).

Charles Wesley understood that many people whose sin has been canceled by God still come under its power. But he assures us:

He breaks the power of canceled sin,
He sets the prisoner free;
His blood can make the foulest clean;
His blood availed for me.

Thousands of people plagued by a sexual past are walking in freedom today, thanks to the power of Christ's blood. The fact of what happened in the past can never be changed, but the power of that past can be diminished.

ACTION STEP

When Christ said, "If your right eye causes you to sin, tear it out and throw it away," He meant we should do whatever is necessary to keep us from falling into sexual sin.

Now is the time to (1) burn those bridges to your past life of sexual failure, (2) become strictly accountable to your counselor, and (3) pursue God passionately, trusting Him to meet the needs that arise deep within the human heart. Begin each day with submission and prayer.

Chapter 8

The Healing Power of Forgiveness

If you are a victim of the misdeeds of someone else, you cannot put your past behind you unless you forgive. And yes, you *can*, by God's grace and with His help, forgive. Indeed, you *must* forgive.

When a Chicago couple took a vacation in the Caribbean and left their children at home to fend for themselves, the city—and for that matter, the nation—was outraged. The children, ages nine to two years, had to exist as best they could amid squalor and a scarce food supply.

These children represent hundreds of thousands of others who are neglected and abused. No matter how many case workers are employed to identify and care for mistreated children, there is always more work to be done. Even as I write, a report has come over the national news saying that child abuse is on the rise. We shudder at what happens behind closed doors.

Our greatest hurts do not come from disease, poverty, or physical pain. Our deepest emotional wounds are inflicted by other people. Proverbs reads, "A man's spirit will endure sickness, but a crushed spirit who can bear?" (18:14). This chapter is for those who have a broken spirit, a spirit that has been crushed by the cruel actions of others.

Enough has been said in this book about the various kinds of broken lives that are all around us. What happens if we do not resolve these emotional roadblocks biblically? Such feelings can lead to a whole cluster of negative emotions.

Some respond by withdrawing into depression, despair, and deep resentment. They build a shell around themselves, determined never to be hurt again. They spend their lives preserving their independence by retreating into their own private world, putting a Do Not Disturb sign on the door of their hearts. They endure long periods of depression. They want to be sure that no one will ever hurt them again.

Others become hard and indifferent, acting out their anger. They say, "I hate my parents, and so I will hate their God." They choose to live in open rebellion, finding their escape through drugs, alcohol, or immorality. If life has not treated them well, they will live it to the full in their own way and on their own terms.

Satan stands by, ready to exploit this emotional turbulence. Thus the feelings of anger and insecurity become inflamed, a passionate force that spirals out of control. And even when the emotions are subdued, the pain erupts unexpectedly.

Those who are bound by anger will use their past as an excuse for every kind of failure and sinful relationship. Confrontation, even if done in love, is often rejected out of hand; they refuse responsibility, since all blame is transferred to those on whom their anger is heaped.

God can speed up the process so that healing takes place more quickly, if we learn to forgive those who have wronged us. In fact, there can be no healing unless we choose to forgive those who have done us evil. Forgiveness is not an easy answer, but it is the only answer if we are serious about dissolving the hostility that is so destructive to our walk with God.

The purpose of this chapter is to understand the basis of forgiveness and show that it is possible to forgive, even if we do not see justice meted out in our lifetime. God uses our willingness to forgive to restore and to heal. We can be comforted with the promise "He heals the brokenhearted and binds up their wounds" (Ps. 147:3). Unfortunately, many do not know that they are fighting a battle that can be won.

Christ knew how difficult it is to forgive, so He gave the disciples specific instructions on how it is to be done. We need such instruction, for it has been correctly said, "He who has never had to forgive has never lived." At a young age we all learned that the world is fundamentally unjust. Successfully coping with injustice is the key to breaking the logjam of hostility and mistrust.

Just after a tender reminder about the value of children and the judgment that awaits those who cause them to stumble, Christ launched into this discussion of forgiveness. Perhaps He was thinking about all those children who would someday have to forgive their parents. Jesus wanted to demonstrate that in our fallen world we cannot live without forgiveness.

Perhaps Matthew was bothered by Peter, who talked too much. James resented John; Philip and Andrew did not see eye to eye. And, of course, there was Judas, who fooled his friends with his piety and ended up betraying Christ. They, like us, needed to be taught the lesson of forgiveness.

CHARACTERISTICS OF FORGIVENESS

"If your brother sins against you, go and tell him his fault, between you and him alone. If he listens to you, you have gained your brother" (Matt. 18:15). If someone has wronged you, your first responsibility is to go to that individual and see if the matter can be resolved. Christians especially should take the initiative to do whatever is necessary to be at peace. To go is difficult; it is easier to spread rumors, to tell others how wrong the offender really is.

Forgiveness Seeks Reconciliation

Christ takes for granted that the offense has taken place within a church setting, where both parties are Christians. Later we shall speak more specifically about those instances outside the church where the offender neither seeks forgiveness nor is willing to extend it.

Of course, we should also go, especially if we are the ones who have done the wrong. As Christians, we should do everything possible to be reconciled with those whom we have offended. We should be the first to say, "I would be very pleased if I could hear you say, 'I forgive you.'" Politely insist on hearing those words; if forgiveness is not extended, you must accept the outcome, realizing that you have done all that you could to tear down the walls of anger.

When we do go to seek reconciliation, Christ will be with us. "For where two or three are gathered in my name, there am I among them" (Matt. 18:20). This promise is often quoted in prayer meetings, and certainly it is true that Christ is with those who gather, no matter how few in number. But in context it is a promise that where two or three are gathered together to seek reconciliation, Christ is there to help bring it about. We should go in faith, praying and hoping that we will be able to "gain our brother."

However, when we set out to resolve a matter our efforts might fail. For one thing, the person might not acknowledge what he did. He might deny it, or reinterpret the events to suit his fancy. Or perhaps if we are the offender, the person whose forgiveness we seek might not give it to us. Reconciliation, even under the best of circumstances, is not easy.

Christ anticipated that the matter might be unresolved, and added, "But if he does not listen, take one or two others along with you, that every charge may be established by the evidence of two or three witnesses" (Matt. 18:16). If this is ineffective, then the offender should be disciplined by the church and treated with respectful avoidance.

Even when forgiveness has been extended and received, there

might be a need for further counsel and follow-up. For example, if a husband has been unfaithful to his marriage, it is not enough for him to simply hear that his wife has chosen to forgive him. Forgiveness might take place in a moment of time, but reconciliation takes much longer. Once trust has been violated, it must be rebuilt. Reconciliation outside of the church context is usually even more difficult. Many people who have not experienced the forgiveness of Christ will find it exceedingly difficult to either extend or accept forgiveness. We have already learned that the more insensitive and calloused the person is, the more unlikely there will be any hope of having a meeting of the minds.

Should we forgive those who have wronged us even if they don't ask for it? How can we forgive those who do not even acknowledge that a wrong was done, or those who have already died? Some Bible teachers, basing their conclusions on Luke, teach that we can only forgive if it is requested. "Pay attention to yourselves! If your brother sins, rebuke him, and if he repents, forgive him, and if he sins against you seven times in the day, and turns to you seven times, saying, 'I repent,' you must forgive him" (Luke 17:3–4).

Certainly it is better when we are asked for forgiveness. However, I believe we can forgive anyone, even those who do not seek it; there is such a thing as one-sided forgiveness, a kind of forgiveness that makes us willing to release our feelings of bitterness to God even if there is no reconciliation with the other person(s). Like Christ on the cross, we can forgive those who have hurt us even if they are not sorry for what they have done. In such instances, forgiveness means that we surrender our resentments to God, choosing to let Him deal with the offender.

"But," someone protests, "I don't even want to forgive the offender. Why should I let him off the hook? I want him to get what he deserves!" We'll answer that objection a bit later, but for now, we have to remind ourselves how costly forgiveness really is. It is hard to forgive because the price tag is so high. Forgiveness is one of the most difficult assignments you will ever be given.

Forgiveness Is Costly

Jewish law taught that you only have to forgive an offender three times. Peter, ever the one to give his spin on the discussion at hand, asked, "Lord, how often will my brother sin against me, and I forgive him? As many as seven times?" (Matt. 18:21). He probably expected to be commended for his loving spirit, but Christ surprised him by saying, "I do not say to you seven times, but seventy-seven times" (v. 22). To forgive seventy-seven times means in effect that we should extend unlimited forgiveness to those who have wronged us.

To better explain why He could expect so much from His followers, Christ told a parable, which in principle had happened many times. "For this reason the kingdom of heaven may be compared to a king who wished to settle accounts with his slaves" (v. 23). You probably know the story. It is the end of the fiscal year, and the king has to take account of his assets. As his servants are giving an account of their year's work, he spies one who is woefully in debt. Incredibly, this servant owed "ten thousand talents" (v. 24).

Although it is difficult to know the value of a talent in the dollar equivalent, it is generally believed to be about $1,000. If you multiply that by 10,000, you will get some $10 million! Of course we don't know how this servant acquired such a massive debt. Perhaps he took the king's money and made foolish investments; maybe he even was a deceitful servant, spending the money for selfish projects and pretending it was being used for something else. Clearly, he was a bad servant, a man who most probably could not be trusted. Either way, there was no argument about how much he owed.

The king thunders, "You scoundrel, you have taken advantage of my generosity; I demand that you and your wife and your children be sold so that I can at least get something back of what is owed me." According to Roman law, the king had the authority to do just that. In prison the man would work, earning a few farthings toward his massive debt.

With a gesture of despair, the servant falls before the king saying, "Have patience with me, and I will pay you everything" (v. 26). Of course he was foolish to think this was possible. Someone has calculated that if he were to work for the basic daily wage of the day it would take him at least three hundred years to repay the debt, assuming that he saved all he made and worked seven days a week! Thankfully, the king did not exercise his prerogative to send the servant to the debtor's prison. He had compassion on the man and "released him and forgave him the debt" (v. 27). Forgiveness is not found in the person forgiven, but in the forgiver. It is an act of grace.

Forgiven!

Was this forgiveness free? Think carefully before you answer. To the forgiven servant it was free, but it was very costly. That year as the king balanced his books he had to absorb the debt; he was short $10 million. He had to make a huge bad-debt entry and take other assets to balance the ledger. A major chunk of his fortune was gone. Forgiveness cost him plenty.

Of course, we should see ourselves in this story. Christ's point is that we owe God more than we will ever know. We have offended His justice and spurned His loving overtures. We might not realize that we are that guilty, but from His standpoint our debt is infinite, for we have nothing with which to pay.

In fact, we are in a worse position than this servant. At least theoretically he might have been able to pay his debt. Perhaps a rich uncle might have died; perhaps he might have won the Roman lottery, if it existed! It was a long shot, but it is conceivable that he might have been able to pull it off.

In our case there is no possibility that we could pay what we owe God. What He demands we have none of; all of our good deeds added from here to eternity would not pay for a single sin. He alone can supply what we need, namely, the gift of His righteousness.

Augustus Toplady had it right:

Could my zeal no respite know,
Could my tears forever flow,
All for sin could not atone;
Thou must save, and Thou alone.[23]

But the good news is that God personally makes the payment. For Him, like the king in the parable, forgiveness is very costly. He loved us so much that He sent His only begotten Son to suffer, bearing our sins so that we might be acquitted. We were not redeemed with silver or gold, "but with the precious blood of Christ, like that of a lamb without blemish or spot" (1 Peter 1:19). The blood of Christ is of more value than all the riches of the world combined. Though it was precious, and we were unworthy, God underwrote the price tag for redemption.

Death and the curse were in our cup
O Christ 'twas full for Thee
But Thou hast drained the last dark drop
'Tis empty now, for me.[24]

Forgiveness Begets Forgiveness

The forgiven servant left the presence of the king with his certificate of pardon clutched in his hand. He could hardly wait to tell his wife how generous the king was! As he turned a corner near his home, he spotted a friend who owed him some money, a hundred denarii to be exact. It was the equivalent of about $20, perhaps three months' wages.

Instantly, the forgiven servant remembered the debt. He had often wondered whether he would see his money again, and now was the time to make sure he would. It was either now or never.

"Pay up!" he shouted.

The startled man, with a gesture of despair, threw himself at the feet of this servant and said, "Have patience with me, and I will pay you" (Matt. 18:29).

You might think that those words would have triggered the forgiven servant's memory. Those were the phrases he had spoken in the presence of the king just hours earlier (v. 26). Having been so generously forgiven, you could expect that he would now, in turn, forgive.

But his heart was as hard as flint. There was no spark of kindness, no ability to set the man free. Instead he had the man sold into debtor's prison "until he should pay the debt" (v. 30). Right is right and wrong is wrong! Justice demanded it, the servant reasoned. Certainly he had a legal right to demand payment, but he did not have a moral right to do so. When we choose to accept forgiveness, we obligate ourselves to practice it.

When his friends heard about the plight of their fellow servant, they were heartbroken. They remembered his wife and family; they knew that the debt should be paid, but it was so small that some negotiation would have been possible. Given enough time the slate could be cleared.

They had no legal means of appeal, so they went directly to the king with their story. Maybe he would think of some way to get the man out of prison. And it might well be that they had already heard how generous the king was with the hard-hearted servant.

When the king heard the news, he was angry. He thought back to his own generosity, his willingness to forgive the hapless man. Incredibly, the man who had been given a new lease on life because of sheer grace would not extend a much smaller measure of grace to someone else.

The king then summoned the forgiven servant and scolded him, "You wicked servant! I forgave you all that debt because you pleaded with me. And should not you have had mercy on your fellow servant, as I had mercy on you?" (vv. 32–33).

And the king handed this servant over to the torturers until he would repay the amount he had been forgiven.

Then Christ adds those startling words, "So also my heavenly Father will do to every one of you, if you do not forgive your brother from your heart" (v. 35).

Let us not think that God withdraws forgiveness once it has been bestowed. In fact, there are good reasons to believe that once a person has trusted Christ as Savior, he will be saved even if he does not remain faithful to his commitment. God's gifts are irrevocable.

Christ is not speaking about the torment of hell; nor is this purgatory. This is the torment of earth, the poison of anger and bitterness that spills into every area of life. God does not revoke His forgiveness, but the unforgiving person pays for his hardheartedness in his own inner spirit. There is a price to be paid for failing to extend the grace to others that God has freely given to us.

LIFE-CHANGING LESSONS ON FORGIVENESS

Here are some lessons on forgiveness with the power to free us so that we might be able to forgive those who have wronged us. These principles help those who have been hurt to take a giant step toward the peace they so desperately need.

Forgiveness Is Costly

We've learned that forgiveness is free to the person who receives it but very costly for the person who dispenses it. The one who does the forgiving must absorb the cost and let the offender go free. For example, Paul said that Christians should not take other believers to court because it is a poor testimony to the people of the world. Then he adds, "Why not rather suffer wrong? Why not rather be defrauded?" (1 Cor. 6:7). To forgive someone who has chiseled you out of your rightful inheritance is costly to you, but it is better than going to court before unbelievers. Paul says we should "take the hit" for our brother, let him have the inheritance that is ours, and let him go free! That is not cheap!

Please read the words of L. Gregory Jones carefully. They just might change your life:

> Unfortunately, the cost of forgiveness is too high for many people. Consequently, they invent and turn to cheaper versions of forgiveness, ones that will enable them to "feel" or "think" better about themselves—or simply to "cope" with their situation—without having to engage in struggles to change or transform the patterns of their relationships.[25]

In another section he writes:

> But Christian forgiveness requires our death, understood in the specific form and shape of Jesus Christ's dying and rising. For as we participate in Christ's dying and rising, we die to our old selves and find a future not bound by the past.[26]

Suppose a husband commits adultery and then asks his wife's forgiveness. She chooses to forgive him, bless her heart. But it is very costly for her; she must bear in her own heart the pain of rejection, the betrayal, and the personal loss. But she says that she is willing to do that for the good of her husband and the relationship. If she did what she felt like doing, she would run him out of the house and tell him he is never welcome again. But she overcomes those emotions and chooses the painful route of forgiveness, which is the first step toward reconciliation. That is a "dying" like that of Christ.

Lies are told about you, and the person responsible eventually comes to ask your forgiveness. You give it to him freely, but you still must pay the cost. The rumors have a life of their own and your reputation is tarnished. You will never be able to contain all of the damage, but you let the offender go free.

If God paid our debt at high personal cost, what makes us think we can pay the debt of someone else without accepting some loss?

Of course, as we shall see, we have much more to gain by forgiveness than we have to lose, but to forgive is to be willing to do what is difficult. It is to set someone free who does not deserve it.

C. S. Lewis put it well, "Every one says forgiveness is a lovely idea, until they have something to forgive."[27]

When We Forgive, We Are Most Like God

Our ability to forgive is based on God's free forgiveness. The reason we can forgive much is because God forgave us much. "Be kind to one another, tenderhearted, forgiving one other, as God in Christ forgave you" (Eph. 4:32). The source of our forgiveness is God's forgiveness.

No matter what wrong has been done against you, it is not as great as our wrongs toward God. If the greatness of the sin is determined by the greatness of the being against whom it is committed, our sins are great indeed.

We often pray, "O God, make me godly"; that is, we want to be more like God. Then we complain when He gives us the opportunity to extend forgiveness. Forgiveness is a necessary course in His curriculum, for it provides an opportunity to be like our Father in heaven, who does good even to evil men.

Forgiveness is not an emotion. It is a choice to make; we can forgive even if we don't feel like it. If you wait until you feel like forgiving, you will not forgive. We must choose against those feelings of bitterness that would like to control our attitude and behavior. God chose to forgive, and so should we.

Through Forgiving, We Ourselves Are Made Free

In this parable the man who refused to forgive his fellow servant was handed "to the torturers until he would repay all that was owed [the king]" (v. 34 NASB). I've already mentioned that this is the torture that is endured on earth by those who do not forgive. These torturers may be demons who are allowed by God to harass those who will not give up their bitterness. No one is more afflicted than those who nurse their anger and resentment.

"The moment I start hating a man I become his slave. He even controls my thoughts. I can't escape his tyrannical grasp on my mind. When the waiter serves me steak it might as well be stale bread and water. The man I hate will not permit me to enjoy it." So wrote S. I. McMillen in the book *None of These Diseases.*[28] Sometimes I say to those who have been mistreated, "Has not the person who has wronged you done enough damage in your life—why do you hold on to this bitterness and let him continue to interfere with your personal joy and freedom?" The best way to be free of his destructive influence is to forgive.

Forgiveness is something good that we do for ourselves. Even if we acted selfishly, we would forgive because it silences the torturers. Even if we cannot, for whatever reason, be reconciled to those who did the wrong, we must forgive for our own benefit. If we continue to be tortured, we will torture others. Just witness the cycle of abuse and manipulation that is perpetuated in a family line. Anger begets anger; forgiveness begets forgiveness.

Even if the person who did the wrong has died, we must forgive. I remember hearing the story of a young man whose mother was a prostitute. He was reared in an atmosphere of guilt, disruption, and shame. But years later, for his own peace of mind, he chose to forgive his mother. By then she had already died, so he took the train all the way from the Midwest to the East Coast to stand at the grave of his mother and let all the hurt spill out. Then he chose to forgive her, to release those feelings of resentment so that he could get on with his life. At that moment he was "godly," that is, exercising the mercy and grace of the God who had saved him.

Having been forgiven, he chose to forgive.

Those who have much to forgive often remind us that letting go of our bitter emotions is both an act and a process. We must consciously forgive, aware that the same feelings of anger and resentment might return again. But within time, the past will lose its power. God will help us to rise to a new day. It begins by saying, "I choose to forgive."

"Forgiveness," said Mark Twain, "is the fragrance that the flower leaves on the heel that crushed it."

Forgiveness Is an Act of Faith

For years I wondered how to answer a young mother who said, "Why should I forgive . . . I'm the one who was wronged . . . he ran off and got married and does not send me child support and left me with the kids . . . why should he go free . . . where is justice?"

Where is justice?

There is an answer for this dear lady and others like her who wonder why they should let someone off the hook who does not deserve such mercy. Thankfully, it is possible to forgive without surrendering our desire for wrongs to be made right and justice to triumph.

Christ taught us the path to follow: "When he was reviled, he did not revile in return; when he suffered, he did not threaten, but continued entrusting himself to him who judges justly" (1 Peter 2:23). Christ was willing to be mistreated without setting the record straight. The angels in heaven were at the ready, waiting for a word from His lips so that they could punish His tormentors and deliver Him from their devices. But Christ was willing to let the Father take care of it. He chose to entrust His case to the Supreme Court, believing that justice would be meted out with precision.

Two thousand years have passed and those who mocked Christ have not yet been brought to trial. But in the Day of Judgment, they will give account for their deeds and get exactly what they deserved; not one mite less and not one mite more.

That's why Christ did not feel the need to "even the score" on earth, though He had the power to do so. He was willing to wait because He had confidence in the Judge of all the earth. In the courtroom of the

King, every case tried on earth will be retried, every secret crime will be revealed, and every action of human beings will come under scrutiny.

When God judges the unconverted, they will justly suffer for their misdeeds, abandoned to their fate. When He judges His people, their sins are laid on Christ, though they will be rewarded in heaven for the deeds "done in the body, whether good or evil" (2 Cor. 5:10). Either way, every wrong will be accounted for. The scales of justice will be balanced.

Either he will personally pay for his misdeeds throughout all of eternity or else his guilt will be borne by Christ. Either way, your situation will come before God and the matter will be correctly resolved. Throughout all of eternity we will sing, "Just and true are Thy ways, Thou King of saints."

You and I can forgive today; we can let those who have wronged us off the hook because we know they are still on God's hook. G. K. Chesterton had a point when he wrote, "Forgiveness means pardoning the unpardonable or it is not forgiveness."

Having accepted God's forgiveness, we are forever obligated to forgive.

ACTION STEP

In an act of faith, choose to forgive the person who has wronged you most deeply. Give your resentment and desire for justice to God. Finally, "let go" of the power of the thoughts that have been replaying in your mind like a worn record.

Chapter 9

Empty Obsessions

A mother struggles with the gruesome thought that she just might kill her baby with a knife. She resists the impulse but does not know whether she can trust herself to be alone with him.

A man has the desire to push a window open, sneak into the bedroom, and rape the woman he knows lives down the street. He has never done it, but he wonders what it would be like to act out his fantasy. He fears that one of these evenings, he just might cross the line and do it.

A father of three small children has uncontrollable fits of anger. After he has smashed dishes against the mirror or put his fist through the wall, he becomes subdued and wonders how he could do such a thing. His wife and children live in terror, not knowing when the next blowup might come. His temper can be triggered by the most trivial matters, though for the most part he is a fine husband and father.

Obsessive-compulsive behavior of various kinds is not new to the human race. Whether it is the woman who resorts to drink or the man who returns to destructive sexual escapades or the teenager who knowingly blows his mind on drugs, humankind has always struggled with the gap between what we know is best and what we actually do. Bizarre behavior in the face of better knowledge is simply a part of the mystery of our fallenness.

A STORY OF TERROR AND HOPE

In the New Testament there is a story about a man who can be best described as an obsessive-compulsive schizophrenic. It is a story of terror and despair, a story of helplessness, but also a story of hope. In the presence of Christ miracles happen.

Let's paint the picture and hang it in the gallery of our minds. The details come together, bit by bit, frame by frame.

Where He Lived: The Tombs

Dusk had settled on the shores of Galilee when Christ arrived on the other side of the lake. Then we read, "They came to the other side of the sea, to the country of the Gerasenes. And when Jesus had stepped out of the boat, immediately there met him out of the tombs a man with an unclean spirit. He lived among the tombs" (Mark 5:1–3). On this eastern side of Galilee was the home of Gentiles who lived in small villages and farms. A desolate area with hills and caves was just a few hundred yards from where Christ's boat came ashore. Once, when I toured Israel, I saw a depressing wasteland with tombs hewn out of barren rocks much like the one Mark describes. The gaping holes are a reminder that this was an ancient cemetery, a place that could properly be visited, but hardly a place where one would want to live. And yet, this man called such a place his home.

In this rough-hewn cemetery, Christ met a demented man. We do not know how long this loner had lived in this wilderness, but there he was—seeking shelter amid the rocks, and above all, isolation. We can imagine him eating scraps of dead fish or chewing on weeds. We're surprised that he stayed alive, but he survived, keeping his distance, staying out of the sight of passersby.

Why was he there? Perhaps he was run out of town and had nowhere else to go. In those days, as in ours, people simply did not know what to do with those whose strange behavior caused them fear.

But then again, it also may be that he preferred to live away from civilization. Those who have experienced the terror of emotional and spiritual distress are uncomfortable in the company of others; their pain is increased in the presence of joy and meaningful communication. They particularly disdain personal discussion, expressions of happiness, and singing.

So perhaps the man *chose* to live here. He chose a place that would correspond to the mood that polluted his body and mind. People with mental disorders often keep their house or apartment in a condition that reflects their own state of mind. They might live in a mess of dirt and smells, a rather accurate barometer of their feelings. Either that or they have an opposite reaction, and opt for compulsive cleanliness, obsessed with the presence of germs and dirt. For this man there was a graveyard within and a graveyard without.

Now we must dip our brush and add another layer to the picture. We must capture him as best we can; we must visualize him in a frenzy of bizarre activity.

How He Acted: Out of Control

"And no one could bind him anymore, not even with a chain, for he had often been bound with shackles and chains, but he wrenched the chains apart, and he broke the shackles in pieces. No one had the strength to subdue him" (vv. 3–4).

When other men tried to wrestle him down, they surely must have known that they were confronting more than just a human being. This man's body appeared to be but a shell for the spirits that inhabited him. He was unpredictable and disordered, continually acting on the basis of his next haphazard impulse. Yes, he was out of control.

Men tried to bind him, perhaps to subdue his wild frenzies, but also to help him. Perhaps they wanted to keep him from hurting himself. Or they might have wanted to make sure he did not harass other families in the village. Whatever their motive, we can be quite sure that they intended to bind him for his good and their protection.

He rejected their help. Perhaps he had good reason to be afraid. Or, he might have misread their motives, repudiating their assistance. A part of him cried for help; another part would have rejected the help that might be offered. The ambiguous behavior of the emotionally wounded is confusing to those who want to help.

Our portrait is still incomplete. We need to capture his face; we need to see the pain, the revulsion, the hopelessness. As best we can, we must look beyond his body to understand the distress of his soul.

We continue painting the picture.

What He Felt: Self-Hate

"Night and day among the tombs and on the mountains he was always crying out and cutting himself with stones" (v. 5). We do not know what he was trying to say as he called out to anyone who was in earshot. Usually he heard only the echo of his own voice. Perhaps he was calling for help, but then again he also may have been uttering words of self-condemnation. He was berating himself for his despair and guilt.

As he cried out, he was cutting himself. Thin streams of blood flowed from his arms, legs, and neck. The scars were a reminder of attempted suicide. Or possibly he sought physical pain, which seemed to compensate for his guilt. Someone had to suffer for his sin and self-condemnation, and his conscience insisted that he be the one.

Until now we have considered only the man. But as we look carefully at the story, we learn that Christ saw beyond the man to the demons who tormented him. Christ was saying, "Come out of the man, you unclean spirit!" (v. 8). And though it was the man who bowed before Christ, in reality it was the demons using the man's vocal cords who said, "What have you to do with me, Jesus, Son of the Most High God? I adjure you by God, do not torment me" (v. 7).

Now we can better understand this man's desperate sense of self-hatred. Satan, who is in control of these demonic spirits, always wants people to feel guilty, unworthy of divine grace. This self-incrimination is a prison that has held many in the grip of devilish bondage. For if we hate ourselves, we cannot feel loved by God. James says that we should not curse men because they are made in the image of God. Nor should we curse ourselves.

If the devil can make us hate our appearance, if he can make us dissatisfied with our lot in life, if he can make us determined to never forgive ourselves for what we have done, nor forgive those who have wronged us—his goals are, for the moment, achieved.

To see God's hatred of sin and our own fallenness is beneficial only if it leads us to a fresh understanding of God's undeserved forgiveness and acceptance. To see ourselves apart from Christ leads only to despair.

Why, we might ask, does Satan try to imprison the soul? Remember, he is angry, viciously angry, at the human race in general and Christians in particular. He was, after all, God's highest creation, His most beautiful angel. He was crowned with beauty and honor. It was his responsibility to make sure that all the praise of other angels would go directly to God. But pride caused him to steal some of that praise.

Never in the universe has a creature fallen so far. But when Satan was able to get Adam and Eve to sin, he thought the whole human race would now have to follow him. Human beings, he assumed, would unite with him in his rebellion against God. He had no idea that God would use this unhappy occasion to display His might and grace. Nor could he foresee the lake of fire where he will spend eternity.

Nor did he know that God had a secret plan by which He would redeem a part of the human race. To add insult to injury, Satan discovered that the redeemed would be exalted far above the honors he once experienced. These creatures whom he incited to sin would be at the right hand of God the Father; they would be made heirs of God and joint heirs with Christ. Christ, the eternal glorious Son of God, would be called their brother!

Satan's resentment is inflamed. He is enraged and filled with vengeance. There is no way for him to attack God directly, so he attacks the human race to get back at God. We cannot live without encountering his resistance and anger.

Back to the story.

Thankfully, we can now pick up our brush and paint a picture of hope. Christ had arrived.

Who He Encountered: Jesus

Notice the interplay between the demons and the personality of the man. Christ was saying, "Come out of the man, you unclean spirit!" (v. 8).

As we have learned, the man bowed before Christ, and in so doing, the demons also bowed before the Lord God. The talking spirit, presumably speaking for the others, begged that they might not be tormented, and Christ asked, "What is your name?" Obviously, He did not ask about the name of the man, but the name of this occult presence.

The demon, ever subject to Christ, answered, "My name is Legion, for we are many" (v. 9). A Roman legion was a regiment of six thousand troops. The man felt as though he had a whole battalion of demons inside of him. In the presence of Christ, the demon could neither lie nor plead silence. Christ had given the command and the demon spoke. And he spoke the truth.

The story continues. "And he begged him earnestly not to send them out of the country" (v. 10). The man was speaking, or at least his voice box was being used, but it was the plea of the demon that was expressed. The lead demon desired to stay in the area and enter into a herd of pigs.

"Send us to the pigs; let us enter them" (v. 12). The demon did not want to exist in a disembodied state. Christ complied. "So he gave them permission. And the unclean spirits came out and entered the pigs; and the herd, numbering about two thousand, rushed down the steep bank into the sea and drowned in the sea" (v. 13).

This was proof that a miracle had indeed happened. People have questioned whether Christ had the right to destroy two thousand pigs that belonged to the farmers in the area. The obvious answer is that Christ owns everything, the cattle on a thousand hills and the pigs on a thousand seashores. No doubt He wanted to dramatize His power in an area that had, for the most part, rejected Him.

If we ask what happened to the demons after the pigs drowned, we can only speculate that they left the animals and were free to roam, awaiting further instructions from their malevolent commander. Their desire to enter animals was granted, though their stay would be brief.

Those who owned the pigs were not happy. "They came to Jesus and saw the demon-possessed man, the one who had had the legion, sitting there, clothed and in his right mind, and they were afraid" (v. 15). Even if they were grudgingly happy for him, they were not happy about their pigs. And with that they urged Christ to leave.

INTERPRETING THIS EXPERIENCE

We wish, of course, that all such stories had a happy ending. All of us know someone who struggles with compulsions that seem to elude rational analysis. Often no cure is available.

If this man had been living today, he would have been put in a psychiatric ward; he would have been given sedatives so that the hospital staff could manage his outbursts. He would have been written off as one who would never be capable of living a normal life. I do not speak critically, since we can be thankful for doctors and nurses who do the best they can with situations that are often well beyond human analysis and cure. Indeed, we've all known people who have not been helped even with the best of Christian counsel.

And yet this story speaks to us today. Before we learn its lessons, we have to confess that there is much here that we cannot understand. And we must be cautious in our analysis.

Not all who experience bizarre behavior have a demon as did this man. Counselors, who know much more than I, tell us that the causes of human behavior are very complex. Sometimes schizophrenics have a chemical imbalance; many of them are helped with the right medication. Then there are those who go through periods of depression or compulsive behavior and come out of the phase for no apparent reason. Though Satan might be involved at various levels of these struggles, we can never fix the blame on him alone and think that an exorcism is all that is needed. The Scriptures never excuse human beings for their actions, even if they are influenced by Satan.

We are also limited in our analysis. We simply do not know why a demon had free rein in this man's life. Was it because the people in this area were worshipers of false gods, and demonic activity was God's judgment? Or had this man personally given himself to Satan, seeking the help of his enemy? Or is it because he sided with Satan in accepting occultism and defiance of God? We simply do not know.

This account should not make us doubt God's protection. Satan could not touch Job without God's express permission. And when Satan came to taunt God one more time, the Almighty gave him more power, but again prescribed the limits. God, not Satan, was in charge of Job's trial. Satan could not even tempt Peter without Christ's permission (Luke 22:31–32).

In this story in the book of Mark we can be sure that this man was not yet a believer in the true God and thus was more vulnerable to demonic attack. If we had all the facts, we would know why Satan was allowed such control over him. We do know that Satan gains a foothold in people's lives most often because of involvement with occult activity or other forms of disobedience.

Satan cannot inflict havoc in the lives of people at will; there must always be a reason, an open door through which he tries to gain some measure of entry. Any sin, whether it be anger, immorality, drugs, or false doctrine, will be exploited by spirits who desire to drive people away from God. There are varying degrees of demonic involvement, beginning with temptation all the way to bizarre obsessions.

Nor can we understand why Christ came to deliver this particular man but evidently bypassed others with similar disorders. Surely this was not the only man in Israel who was demonized, living in self-imposed isolation. Today we know there are many people in similar situations who have not experienced a dramatic deliverance.

Though we have few answers to our questions, we are left with a story of hope, a story that reminds us that when demons and Christ have a confrontation, Christ always wins. Here is a story that inspires us to believe in Christ's ability to deliver and transform. It is a story that introduces us to our conflict with the spirit world.

THE LESSONS TO BE LEARNED

The apostle Peter knew firsthand how deceptive Satan could be. He never forgot his cowardice when a servant girl accused him of being one of Christ's followers. To encourage people to learn from his mistakes, he warned us that Satan was like a lion: "Be sober-minded; be watchful. Your adversary the devil prowls around like a roaring lion, seeking someone to devour. Resist him, firm in your faith, knowing that the same kinds of suffering are being experienced by your brotherhood throughout the world" (1 Peter 5:8–9). Lions hunt by surprising their victims. They pounce hard at an unexpected moment.

And yet this lion is no match for another Lion, the "Lion of the tribe of Judah" who has in his hands the title deed for the universe (Rev. 5:5). This Lion will not allow Satan to harass us above what we are able to bear. Christ stands with us, encouraging through His promises, strengthening, protecting.

Let us be encouraged.

Sought by Christ

First, we should be reassured by the fact that Christ comes to find us. The demonized man of Galilee was not looking for Christ. The Lord came to this side of the lake at the right time and landed at the right spot. Christ knew that there was a man who desperately needed Him. There in the region of death the Son of God came with a message of life.

If you are a believer in Christ, it is because He sought you and you have been found. We can be grateful that Christ came looking for us, though we were not looking for Him. He defined His job description: "For the Son of Man came to seek and to save the lost" (Luke 19:10).

Now that He has found us, He walks with us through the caves of our past. We do not have to lift every board and overturn every stone on our own. The man in the Gerasenes did not know about Christ, but you and I do. We can invite Him into the caverns of our lives; we can let Him expose the hidden things of darkness and shine His light on our dark side. The promise is, "If you abide in my word, you are truly my disciples, and you will know the truth, and the truth will set you free" (John 8:31–32).

Christ had intimate knowledge of this demonized man long before they met on the other side of Galilee. Just so, Christ knows all about us. You might not know all that has happened to you and why, but Christ knows the whole story of your life from beginning to end. He is the Savior who seeks and finds.

Protected by the Power of Christ

Second, Christ has undisputed authority over the spirit world. When He commanded the demon to speak, the demon spoke; when He commanded the demon and his hordes to leave, they did. They knew who He was, and they knew who they were. He was the Creator; they, the creatures.

Moment by moment, Satan and his hosts can only do what God lets them do and not one whit more. They cannot tempt, coerce, demonize, or harass us unless God gives them approval to do so. What this means is that we need not be overwhelmed by their presence as long as we remember that they have all the limitations of creatures.

Christ's ascension is proof of His infinite superiority over satanic forces. God raised Him up and "seated him at his right hand in the heavenly places, far above all rule and authority and power and dominion, and above every name that is named, not only in this age but also in the one to come" (Eph. 1:20–21).

Christ's victory is unquestioned, but we have mixed results as we confront Satan. Yet, we have the right to share in Christ's victory because we are seated "with him in the heavenly places" (Eph. 2:6). But Satan does not want us to see ourselves as being in heaven; he hopes we will see ourselves as earthbound and helpless. Your situation is not unique. No matter what your struggle, Christ has triumphed, and that gives us hope.

Cleansed by Christ

Third, Satan's uncleanness must be countered by Christ's cleansing and purity. These demonic spirits were aptly called "unclean." Some of these beings evidently specialize in one kind of impurity, others in another. But uncleanness is Satan's trademark. As we have learned, these spirits had to leave when in the presence of someone stronger than they. They would rather enter unclean pigs than stand in the presence of the pure and holy Son of God.

Often people ask, "How can I know whether my particular problem is demonic?" Most of the time it is impossible to tell for one good reason: Demons simply prefer to do their work by strengthening the sins that you and I are willing to tolerate and excuse. Thus often we cannot tell where our own sinful nature ends and where demonic activity begins. Fortunately, it is usually not necessary to make these distinctions, for the answer for both is the same—repentance, cleansing, and faith.

James wrote, "Submit therefore to God. Resist the devil, and he will flee from you. Draw near to God, and he will draw near to you. Cleanse your hands, you sinners, and purify your hearts, you double-minded" (James 4:7–8). The pure heart is the remedy for the unclean feelings and unclean spirits.

Through confession and faith we are delivered from the impurity that plagues our souls, the environment in which evil spirits do their most devastating work.

This is the message we have heard from him and proclaim to you, that God is light, and in him there is no darkness at all. . . . If we walk in the light, as he is in the light, we have fellowship with one another, and the blood of Jesus his Son cleanses us from all sin. (1 John 1:5, 7)

Whatever the condition of your conscience, Christ can cleanse you and free you from self-condemnation. And when your soul is cleansed, the accusations of Satan must subside.

Freedom from Satan's Lies

Fourth, Satan's strategy against us is always based on lies. Because this story does not give us many details, we do not know what lies this man in the tombs believed. But Christ said of Satan, "He was a murderer from the beginning, and does not stand in the truth, because there is no truth in him. When he lies, he speaks out of his own character, for he is a liar and the father of lies" (John 8:44).

Here are some lies that people believe today.

Lie #1: *"I've messed up so badly God cannot give me a proper sense of self-worth and value."*

The issue is not how much we have sinned (terrible as that might be) but rather the greatness of God's undeserved favor toward us.

Lie #2: *"God does not love me."*

"Did God actually say, 'You shall not eat of any tree in the garden'?" (Gen. 3:1). These are the first words Satan ever spoke to a human being, words that questioned the character of God.

We've all been disappointed with God. But when this causes us to turn away from Him, we pay a high price. We undercut the possibility of healing and help. Satan's premise is quite correct, that when we do not believe that God loves us, we will not be able to trust Him.

Lie #3: *"I have to serve the devil because my behavioral ruts are so deep."*

Even Christians have been known to hear accusing voices: "How can you call yourself a Christian after what you've done? God hates you." Satan's desire is to separate believers from their heavenly Father by destroying their fellowship with Him.

These lies must not only be fought through embracing God's promises, but also by making praise a daily habit. Giving thanks to God for our struggles (though not for our sins) will give us the faith and perspective we need to hold our ground. Paul wrote, "In all circumstances take up the shield of faith, with which you can extinguish all the flaming darts of the evil one" (Eph. 6:16). Faith in Christ's present triumph will enable us to fight successfully.

Return to Dignity

Finally, Christ restores our dignity. This demon-possessed man's friends could hardly believe what they saw, and it bears repeating.

"They came to Jesus and saw the demon-possessed man, the one who had had the legion, sitting there, clothed and in his right mind, and they were afraid" (Mark 5:15).

Understandably, this man wanted to follow Jesus. But our Lord had a different idea. "'Go home to your friends and tell them how much the Lord has done for you, and how he has had mercy on you.' And he went away and began to proclaim in Decapolis how much Jesus had done for him, and everyone marveled" (vv. 19–20).

Christ does not come to us today along the shores of Galilee; He does not come in the flesh to confront our demons and turn us into instant evangelists, though we should not think that this is impossible. Christ has committed to the church strength to do His work, to "set the captives free."

You have a right to walk out of any prison that Satan has created for you. In Christ, we can be "free indeed."

ACTION STEP

Read Ephesians 6:10–20 as a prayer to God. In faith accept the pieces of armor as yours. These are not so much "put on" as they are a lifestyle.

When you believe you are attacked by Satan, use the Scriptures against him, even as Christ did. With joy affirm the triumph of Christ over the evil one.

Chapter 10

Channeling God's Power

Back in 1968, together with several other young men, I climbed to the top of Masada, the massive fortification in Israel near the southern end of the Dead Sea. It took us several hours in 100+ degree heat to make it to the top (most tourists now go up in a cable car). By climbing it ourselves, we better understood why the Roman armies were unable to capture the Jews who occupied the top of this fortification. Whenever the Romans tried to scale the mountain, they were beaten back by the Jews, who would simply let rocks roll down on them.

Though greatly outnumbered and with few resources, the Jews lived on the top of the mountain for more than three years before the fortress finally fell to the Romans.

Masada is a stronghold, most likely the fortification referred to as the "strongholds of Engedi" (1 Sam. 23:29). Whoever occupied it had a tremendous advantage over the enemy. All the odds were against the attackers, who found it nigh impossible to scale the mountain with its walls and defenses. Little wonder the Romans had such difficulty laying siege to the fortress. The conflict of Masada teaches us two important principles of warfare. First, it is much easier to defend territory in our possession than to recapture it after it has gone into the hands of the enemy. The Jews kept the Romans at bay for several years, but once Rome captured the fortress, the battle seemed insurmountable.

The analogy is clear. It is much easier to defend ourselves from Satan's attacks than it is to take territory back that we have lost to him. To say no to alcohol is easy if you have never tasted it, but it is much more difficult once it has become a part of your lifestyle. Those who struggle with overeating know how difficult it is to take off some pounds—how much better to have never put them on!

However powerful sexual temptation may be, its attraction will become still stronger after we give in to it. Every time we say yes to our lusts, we develop a natural momentum to say yes later on.

This principle is a powerful reminder that the best (and easiest) time to say no to a sinful lifestyle is when it is first presented to us. No matter how fierce the struggle, every loss means the struggle ahead will be even greater. For every inch we give to Satan, he wants a yard. And every inch we wish to recapture involves serious confrontation with the enemy.

Many of you reading these pages have long since left the days when your life was free from enemy control. Satan (in league with the flesh) has occupied a considerable part of your body and mind for some time. You must recapture the territory that is behind enemy lines.

The same applies to those of you who were abused in your past; the part of you that is ruining your future needs to be reclaimed for the glory of God. The fortresses that hold past memories and feelings must be vacated to make room for the new ownership.

Second, Masada teaches us that to capture enemy fortifications, we must have weapons and personnel equal to the task. Even if the enemy is relatively weak, when he is in a good position, he can do a lot of damage.

If he has entrenched himself, built buttresses, and dug deep foundations, you are set for a long battle. He will not budge, no matter what.

How do we recapture territory that is in enemy hands? How is it possible to go behind enemy lines, dislodge the bulwarks, and route the adversary? How can we plant Christ's flag of victory on territory presently in the midst of enemy occupation?

The answer: Through strong, aggressive prayer. We must be able to access the power of God and focus the victory of Christ directly on the strongholds of the mind and the emotions. This is not the time for general petitions ("Please bless John"); it is the time for strategic warfare with artillery directed toward key targets. We're talking about bombing the ramparts; we are speaking of assaulting the foe and engaging him in direct combat. We are crossing enemy lines, naming the opposing warriors, and taking authority over the intruders. We are in it to win.

This kind of prayer enables us to channel the power of God. We take the victory of the cross, the resurrection, and the ascension and apply it to specific areas of our lives. Through prayer, God's power can halt the setbacks of the past and give hope for the future.

Some New Agers tell us that certain gifted individuals called *channelers* can tap into spiritual power and communicate with "masters of wisdom" who lived on the earth many years ago. They are quite right in insisting there is a spiritual dimension to the universe, but unfortunately they are plugged into the wrong spirit world.

However, I am not prepared to surrender the word *channeling* to the New Agers. Christians are channelers too—channelers for the power of God. There's an old hymn called "Channels Only." Just as a television set can be tuned to different channels, so we can be tuned to God's frequency, and when that happens, lives are permanently changed.

How can we pray in such a way that we will see the unmistakable evidence of changed lives? How can the wounds of the past be healed and the future be made productive?

OBSTACLES TO EFFECTIVE PRAYER

After Paul described the armor of God that all of us must wear if we are to be successful against the enemy, he added: "[Pray] at all times in the Spirit, with all prayer and supplication. To that end, keep alert with all perseverance, making supplication for all the saints" (Eph. 6:18).

This kind of praying has several characteristics which we will examine, but first we must deal with two obstacles, two mental barriers that keep us from meaningful prayer.

Doubting God's Care

The first barrier is that we honestly doubt whether God cares. After all, if He really is as concerned as the Bible seems to teach, where is He when we are sick, when we lose our jobs, or when our family falls apart? As we have already learned, children who have been abused have a difficult time trusting in the care of God.

This is not an easy barrier to overcome, but many people who have been abused or who have suffered injustices have come to grips with their distrust of God and found Him to be a reliable friend. David wrote, "He does not forget the cry of the afflicted" (Ps. 9:12).

I urge you to come to God with your spiritual and emotional bruises and with your misgivings, and you will find that He does heal the brokenhearted and give comfort to those who mourn. Don't think you have to resolve all your doubts and misgivings before you come.

Confusion About God's Will

A second barrier that keeps us off our knees is the thorny problem of the will of God. The Bible says if we ask according to His will, He hears us; but the $64,000 question is, "How do I know what His will is?" We've all thought we knew God's will and prayed accordingly—only to be disappointed. So we gave up, reasoning, "If it is God's will, He will do it whether or not I pray; if it is not God's will, He is not going to do it no matter how hard I pray—so what's the use?"

The net result is that we often pray in unbelief. We mention various matters to God but would be shocked if we saw an answer. We are not convinced He cares, and we don't want to waste energy that will not get results.

In John Bunyan's *The Pilgrim's Progress,* a young woman and her children are seen knocking on the Wicket Gate. In a moment a ferocious dog begins to bark, making the woman and children afraid. They face a dilemma: If they continue to knock, they must fear the dog; if they turn away, the gatekeeper will be offended, and they will not be admitted. They continue to knock ever so fervently. Finally, they hear the voice of the gatekeeper asking, "Who is there?" and instantly the dog ceases barking.

The moment we are serious about prayer, a thousand dogs begin to bark. If we listen to them, we will turn away. If we continue to knock, we will hear the voice of our Master and we will be encouraged to press on.

CHARACTERISTICS OF EFFECTIVE PRAYER

In the next few pages, we will discuss some of the characteristics of effective prayer—but it is up to each individual to put the principles into practice.

We Must Pray in God's Will

When we pray for a promotion, or that a child will be healed, or that God will give us a marriage partner, the question of the will of God always emerges as a part of the picture. In instances like these we must end our prayer with "if it be Thy will."

On the other hand, there are some requests we can make with

absolute certainty that we are praying in His will. We can pray powerfully, without a hint of unbelief. We can pray with boldness and confidence—no need to waffle about the will of God. For example, consider Paul's prayer for the believers in Ephesus.

> I pray that the eyes of your heart may be enlightened, so that you will know what is the hope of His calling, what are the riches of the glory of His inheritance in the saints, and what is the boundless greatness of His power toward us who believe. (Eph. 1:18–19 NASB)

That is the will of God for every believer. No wonder Paul could pray with such confidence!

We Must Exercise Ourselves Unto Godliness

A second example is Colossians 1:9–12, where Paul prays that the believers will have seven special qualities.

> And so, from the day we heard, we have not ceased to pray for you, asking that you may be filled with the knowledge of his will in all spiritual wisdom and understanding, so as to walk in a manner worthy of the Lord, fully pleasing to him: bearing fruit in every good work and increasing in the knowledge of God; being strengthened with all power, according to his glorious might, for all endurance and patience with joy; giving thanks to the Father, who has qualified you to share in the inheritance of the saints in light.

Exercise #1: *Know the will of God.*

This has to do with the wisdom we need to make decisions, the ability to distinguish the good from the best and the false from the true.

Exercise #2: *Walk worthy of the Lord.*

This means that we live lives that are a credit to Christ. The word *worthy* means "weighty"; that is, our lives should make a lasting, indelible impression. Some people's lives are like the sand that is soon washed away. In the end there is nothing left. Paul prayed that the Colossian Christians would live in such a way as to make a permanent impact on others.

Exercise #3: *Bear fruit in every good work.*

This quality involves spiritual productivity. We will bear either good fruit or evil fruit. The fruit that we allow God to develop in our lives will remain. It will not rot when the sun beats on it.

Exercise #4: *Increase in the knowledge of God.*

The pinnacle of all intellectual and spiritual experience is knowing God. We should pray that people would have an increasing understanding of His attributes and of their relationship with Him.

Exercise #5: *Be strengthened spiritually.*

The source for this is nothing less than "His glorious might."

Exercise #6: *Attain spiritual stability.*

We need steadfastness and patience when we encounter the various trials of life.

Exercise #7: *Give thanks.*

Paul viewed this activity as particularly important because it honors the Father, "who has qualified you to share in the inheritance of the saints in light." If you are a woman, think of what it would be like to be married to a man who has all of these qualities! If you are a man, think of having a wife like this!

This is a picture of a person who is emotionally and spiritually whole. Here is one who is no longer a slave to the past, nor held hostage to any damaging effects of a dysfunctional family. Is there any doubt in your mind that this is God's will for every Christian?

Warfare praying (to be explained more fully later), like these prayers of Paul, can be prayed with unswerving confidence. It is praying in line with God's revealed desires. No need to be timid because of uncertainty about God's will.

We Must Pray in the Power of the Spirit

The Holy Spirit is deeply involved in our active prayer life. At times each of us wonders why we have to bother to pray. God could take care of our petitions whether we prayed them or not. We pray that God will heal a sick friend or help a friend overcome an addiction. Why does God wait for us to pray before He acts?

Suppose you have a rebellious, strong-willed six-year-old son and you tell him, "Please do not watch TV this afternoon." He disobeys you.

You decide you are going to wait for him to initiate a discussion about his disobedience. To get his attention, you choose not to prepare dinner for him. Six o'clock comes and nothing is on the table. He is too rebellious to ask for something to eat because such a request is a form of submission—and he is too independent just yet. Of course you could go ahead and make supper anyway—you have the power to do so—but you have a different agenda. The boy's attitude toward his disobedience is of more immediate concern than his hunger.

Around nine o'clock he grudgingly asks if you could fix him something to eat. You are glad he has made this initial step toward you, but you are still not satisfied. His defiance is at the top of your agenda. He isn't ready for his dinner yet.

Of course God could grant us our requests whether we asked or not, or whether we were in fellowship with Him or not—but He has other priorities. First, He wants us to face all areas of disobedience when we make a request before Him: "If I had cherished iniquity in my heart, the Lord would not have listened" (Ps. 66:18).

I do not wish to imply that all of our prayers would be answered if we just surrendered our self-will. My point is that God wants us to pray before He acts simply because our personal relationship with Him is so high on His list of priorities.

His second priority is fellowship with us—His love for us and our love for Him. To pray in the Spirit means we pray in submission and faith, with no unconfessed sin and believing that God will respond to us. "Without faith it is impossible to please him, for whoever would draw near to God must believe that he exists and that he rewards those who seek him" (Heb. 11:6). Thus, in faith, we receive the Spirit's power for effective prayer.

There are some things God will not do until His people pray. As already mentioned, He could act whether we pray or not, and sometimes He does. Yet most important is our attitude toward Him; He wants us to have fellowship with Him. This is number one on His list of objectives. Archbishop Trench said, "Prayer is not overcoming God's reluctance; it is laying hold of His highest willingness."

We come with our need for health, money, and other blessings, and we discover that we have a much greater need—the need for God Himself. The other problems God has allowed in our lives are just vehicles to get us into His presence.

In fact, the Holy Spirit is so vitally concerned about our prayers that in those times when we don't know how to pray—when the hurts are too deep or the matters are too confused—He prays along with us, and He intercedes for us:

> Likewise the Spirit helps us in our weakness. For we do not know what to pray for as we ought, but the Spirit himself intercedes for us with groanings too deep for words. And he who searches hearts knows what is the mind of the Spirit, because the Spirit intercedes for the saints according to the will of God. (Rom. 8:26–27)

Bunyan wrote: "In prayer it is better to have heart without words than words without heart."

What does "praying in the Spirit" mean? It means that we pray in harmony with God. We are not coming with a request simply because we have been pushed into a corner. We are coming to ask but also to love, to fellowship, and to enjoy God. Then the Holy Spirit guides us in our prayer life.

Why not pray right now and ask the Holy Spirit to give you wisdom and guidance in your prayer life? Sometimes we have not because we ask not.

We Must Pray in the Name of Christ

"Truly, truly, I say to you, whatever you ask of the Father in my name, he will give it to you. Until now you have asked nothing in my name. Ask, and you will receive, that your joy may be full" (John 16:23–24).

Why did Christ insist that all prayer had to be in His name? Simply put, we do not have the qualifications we need to approach God, much less receive answers from Him. Here we are totally dependent on Christ's credentials.

Through His name we receive the *access* of Christ. Obviously Christ is in God's presence, and when we pray in His name, we are in God's presence, too. It's not just that God hears us, but He also welcomes us—Christ has ushered us into the presence of the King. Also, we receive the *authority* of Christ. By this I do not mean to say that we have as much authority and power as Christ. If we did, I'm sure we would banish Satan from the face of the earth! But we do have all the authority we need for ourselves; we have the authority we need to be free of demonic control.

The subject of this chapter is how to destroy strongholds—to demolish the power of the enemy. We've learned that effective warfare means we have the resources not just to resist the enemy, but also to rout him from his entrenched positions. This can be done only in the name of someone stronger than Satan, stronger than our past, our sins, and our memories.

In chapter 7 the emphasis was on the victory of Christ over the world of evil spirits. There can be no doubt in our minds about the fact that Satan has been crushed. To pray in Christ's name is to apply His victory boldly in a specific situation.

When Edmund Gravely died at the controls of his small plane, his wife kept the plane aloft for two hours. She radioed for help and her distress signal was picked up, but communication was impossible because she kept changing channels. Eventually she made a rough landing, but it would have been so much easier if she had stayed tuned to the right frequency.

There is only one way to see answers to prayer, and that is to stay tuned to the right channel all day. Every single situation must be brought before our heavenly Father with confidence in the name of the Lord Jesus Christ.

We Must Confront the Enemy

Standing against Satan to undo the damage he has caused is not easy, but it is both necessary and rewarding. The strategy, remember, is to go behind enemy lines to subdue and dislodge him and to send him fleeing.

Remember these simple rules:

Rule #1: *Get suited for the battle.*

We must make sure we are ready for the battles that will face us the minute we are serious about taking authority over the enemy. We must be dressed for the occasion. Through prayer we must put on the "whole armor of God." Mark Bubeck, in his helpful book *The Adversary,* gives an example of the kind of prayer that suits us for battle. A portion of it is given here.

Heavenly Father, I desire to be obedient by being strong in the Lord and the power of Your might. I see that this is Your will and purpose for me. I recognize it is essential to put on the armor that You have provided, and I do so now with gratitude and praise that You have provided all I need to stand in victory against Satan and his kingdom. Grant me wisdom to discern the tactics and sneakiness of Satan's strategy against me. Enable me to wrestle in victory against the princes, powers, rulers, and wicked spirits who carry the battle of darkness against me.

I delight to take the armor You have provided and by faith to put it on as effective protection against the spiritual forces of darkness.

I confidently take the loin girdle of truth that You offer me. I take Him who is the truth as my strength and protection. I reject Satan's lies and deceiving ways to gain advantage against me. Grant me discernment and wisdom to recognize the subtle deceiving ways in which Satan seeks to cause me to accept his lies as truth.[29]

The prayer continues, listing all the pieces of armor, affirming each in faith and accepting each as protection against Satan's strategy. In this way we can arm ourselves for the conflict.

Where territory has been given over to Satan, specific sins must be renounced. Often believers fail to realize it is possible for a sin that has been forgiven to still have control over an individual. Breaking "the power of canceled sin," as Charles Wesley put it, is essential.

Enlisting the prayer support of other believers is also necessary if spiritual hindrances (strongholds) are to be overcome and torn down.

Rule #2: *Begin to pray for others.*

We can now pray for others that they might be brought to submission to God so that their lives will not be destroyed by the prince of destroyers. Again, Bubeck gives an example of that kind of prayer. The following is a helpful summary of a portion of it.

> Loving heavenly Father, in the name of our Lord Jesus Christ, I bring before You [name of other person] in prayer. I ask for the Holy Spirit's guidance that I might pray in the Spirit as You have told me. In the name of the Lord Jesus Christ and as a priest of God, I ask for mercy and forgiveness for the sins of [name] by which he has grieved You. . . . I claim back the ground of his life which he has given to Satan by believing the enemy's deception. In the name of the Lord Jesus Christ, I resist all of Satan's activity to hold [name] in blindness and darkness . . .
>
> I pull down the strongholds formed against [name]. I destroy all those plans formed against [his] mind, his will, his emotions, and his body . . .
>
> I claim [name] for You in the name of the Lord Jesus Christ, and I thank You for the answer to my prayer. In the name of the Lord Jesus Christ, I joyfully lay this prayer before You in the worthiness of His completed work. Amen.[30]

Since God might be using Satan in people's lives to bring them to repentance, we must pray that this would be brought about.

Satan will flee once the person himself has come to the point of cooperation and submission to God. Then we can give specific instructions as to how to pray—developing the concepts of confession, the power we have through our union with Christ, and praise for spiritual victory.

This kind of praying eventually will overcome the resistance of the enemy. Warfare praying is like pounding the walls of a stronghold with artillery designed to smash those walls. Through this kind of believing prayer, we can indeed go behind enemy lines and take back ownership that has either willingly or unwillingly been given to the enemy.

How long do we need to pray before we see results? Sometimes there are immediate changes; sometimes it takes longer. Fasting should also become a part of this kind of intercession. Today when we call a feast, everyone comes, even those whom we have not seen in years. But when we call a fast, the attendance is meager, if anyone shows up at all. Yet Christ assumed we would exercise this discipline:

> "When you fast, do not look gloomy like the hypocrites, for they disfigure their faces that their fasting may be seen by others. Truly, I say to you, they have received their reward." (Matt. 6:16)

Although the disciples had great success casting out demons, there was one particularly stubborn one. The victim was a young boy, and an evil spirit kept throwing him into the fire or into the water. The disciples could not cast the demon out. Christ rebuked them for their unbelief; and later, when the disciples asked why they couldn't cast it out, Christ answered, "This kind does not go out except by prayer and fasting" (Matt. 17:21 NASB).

Perseverance is a word we need to hear often in these days of pop religion and instant solutions. Nothing will accomplish permanent results like persistent, bold, authoritative prayer. Prevailing prayer wins great victories, but the outcome should never be taken for granted. Only when we are under Christ's authority can we exercise that authority as His representatives.

We know we have destroyed a fortress when there is nothing in ourselves (or others for whom we pray) that belongs to the enemy. "Prayer," someone has said, "is not preparation for the work; it *is* the work."

Keeping our eyes on God and our artillery on the enemy is the sure path to victory.

"The prayer of a righteous person has great power as it is working" (James 5:16).

ACTION STEP

Compose a prayer comprised of verses of Scripture that combine worship and submission and invoke protection from the evil one. Pray this Scripture back to God, affirming your desire to walk in obedience to God's will.

Then pray the same prayer for a relative or friend. Pray similar prayers daily, expecting God to answer since you are praying in His will.

Chapter 11

Finding
Your Way Back

Taking a wrong road sometimes has dire consequences. Four of us learned that the hard way back in 1974. Our friends had invited us to spend a few days with them in their new home in northern Wisconsin. One evening in the dead of winter they decided to take us out for dinner to a restaurant in a small, secluded town about ten miles away. Though new in the area, they had confidence they could find it without any trouble.

About five miles down the road they became increasingly convinced that we were on the wrong country road. The car made fresh, deep ruts in the snow; the farther we went, the deeper the snow and the bleaker the surroundings. Clearly we were headed for no-man's-land.

On and on we drove until we came to a crossroads, where we attempted a turnaround. We were stuck in the snow for about an hour and a half in zero-degree temperature, but eventually we managed to get the vehicle back on the road and headed for home.

A wrong turn on the road of life is also hazardous, fraught with numerous unhappy consequences. King David illustrates what can happen when we turn at a wrong corner. You recall that he committed adultery with Bathsheba. Bible scholars hold different views on this story. Some argue that Bathsheba was unaware of the nature of David's request and was therefore coerced. Others argue that she was not only aware of what he wanted when he summoned her, but that she was intentional in trying to bind herself to David for a better life. Ultimately, the text does not tell us, but we can agree that David, as the one in authority and with greater responsibility as the king of Israel, is more at fault. After this, David murdered her husband as part of a cover-up. From there, his life went from bad to worse.

LESSONS ALONG THE ROAD OF LIFE

There are several parallels between our experience in northern Wisconsin and those costly detours along the road of life. Here are some lessons that all of us must learn about heading in the wrong direction.

We Lose Time That Can Never Be Regained

We never did get to that restaurant—in fact, my wife and I have not been there to this day. We had wasted so much time on the wrong road that it was too late to go out to eat; we were just glad we made it home where we could enjoy a bowl of hot soup.

The lesson of wrong roads was a costly one for David—he lost several years of service for his Lord, thanks to the wrong turns he made on his earthly journey. He never could make up for the lost time.

Live for yourself, and you can never go back to that day when you got off course. A ticking clock can be thrown into a trash can, and a current calendar can be burned, but time moves relentlessly forward.

The Ruts We Leave Can Mislead Others

We do not know whether the trail we left in the snow sent a misleading signal to other drivers, but it might have. I can easily imagine someone choosing to follow that road because it looked traveled. Not unreasonably, he could have thought it would lead to the nearby town.

We had the good fortune of turning around and making it back home, but a driver who followed us might not have been that fortunate. He could have decided to go several miles farther only to get stuck and be unable to return at all. He could have been stranded in sub-zero temperatures for quite a long time.

David repented of the path he had chosen, but his children who followed him did not repent of theirs. The two sins of immorality and murder overshadowed his family when he was still alive and continued to do so long after his death. Amnon, David's son, raped his own half-sister, Tamar. Absalom committed immorality with his father's concubines on a rooftop for all to see. Immorality was rampant among David's children.

God had said the sword would not depart from David's household, and it didn't. Absalom was slain by David's military leader, and another son, Adonijah, was killed because he conspired to take his father's throne.

The story is familiar—a man leaves his wife and children to marry a spurious lover, and years later he comes to repent of his sin. His life is turned around and again headed in God's direction, but the children follow the father's path to its destructive end. He changes his direction, but they do not.

The Mistake Cannot Be Corrected by Taking Adjacent Roads

We made a few turns en route to that little town, but because we were on the wrong road to begin with, making a series of different turns only meant we were getting farther from where we wanted to go.

One fork in the road usually leads to another—and when we first choose a wrong path, the next choice also will lead us astray. All roads going in the wrong direction are equally misleading; going from one to another does not get us back on the right path.

Let's return to King David. After he discovered Bathsheba was pregnant with his child, he should have brought Uriah home from battle and admitted candidly what had happened. Then he could have humbly sought Uriah's forgiveness and discussed what his responsibility should be in light of the impending birth of the baby. In this way, David would have repented soon after he took the wrong turn on the highway of life.

But he did what we so often do—he chose to take other paths in a vain attempt to correct his mistake. Unfortunately, those choices only got him further away from where he got off course.

First, he tried Plan A. He brought Uriah home from battle and tried to persuade him to go home, hoping he would make love with his wife, and thus the identity of the child's father would be hidden. But Uriah wouldn't go home. He said it was unfair for him to have such a vacation while his comrades were engaged in war.

Plan B. *I'll get Uriah drunk. Maybe he'll go home then. What he won't do sober, he might do drunk.* That scheme didn't work either.

Parenthetically, we might ask, "Suppose the cover-up had worked—would David have been off the hook?" Hardly. Bathsheba knew the truth, David knew the truth, and, most important, God knew.

Plan C. David's trump card. *I will have Uriah killed.* Then David could take Bathsheba as his wife and everyone (if they could be trusted not to count the months between the wedding and the birth of the baby) would think the child was conceived in wedlock. So he gave Uriah a sealed note to give to Joab, his military commander. It stated that Uriah should be put into the hottest battle, and the other men were to retreat, leaving Uriah to certain death. Joab did as he was asked. Uriah died in battle, and David married Bathsheba.

These decisions actually compounded the original problem. Rather than returning to where he got off course, David's taking these adjacent roads only made it more difficult for him to return. Every mile in the wrong direction meant another mile to cover on the way back.

Of course he could never go back in time, but he could have returned in spirit to where he was before the adultery took place. Eventually he did, but how much better if he had done it sooner rather than later!

Every day we postpone repentance we find ourselves entangled with more sin. Many a knotted mess could be avoided if the participants would only turn around immediately, just as soon as they become conscious of getting off course.

If you need to return to God, today will be as easy as it will ever get. Every day you live, turning around becomes more difficult. The more painful your past, the harder it is to contemplate turning to God. Yet the more necessary it is to do just that.

There Is No Convenient Place to Turn Around

After we had driven five or six miles in the deep snow, we debated whether we should turn around—we thought surely the road must lead to some village or town, or perhaps there would be a farmhouse just around the corner. We had gone so far that we felt the urge to continue, no matter what. The road became narrower, though, and the snow deeper. Still, there was no sign of civilization. Eventually, it appeared we couldn't turn around if we wanted to.

I've known people who pursue destructive paths with abandon. Some are non-Christians who have shut God out of their lives for many years. Even when they come to die, they reject Him. They say, "I have lived without Him; I shall die without Him."

Christians who have been pursuing their own selfish agenda also find it hard to turn around. They have made too many investments along the path of life—they have nursed too many hurts, have sinned too many times, or have felt too much pain. They turn their back toward God and keep going, thinking, "Someday I'll turn around." Yet no time ever seems convenient, no place ever seems appropriate, and, in the end, it is nearly always too late.

David was out of fellowship with God for several months before he was willing to come clean and honestly face his sin and its consequences. In Psalm 32, he describes the agony of those deceptive months.

For when I kept silent, my bones wasted away
through my groaning all day long.
For day and night your hand was heavy upon me;
my strength was dried up as by the heat of summer.
(Ps. 32:3–4)

There were two reasons David found it so hard to turn around. First, his guilt and shame made honest disclosure difficult; and second, he knew that, even though he would be forgiven, the damage of the past could never be made right.

David knew it did not matter how many tears he shed; Bathsheba's purity could never be restored. No matter how many years he lived with regret, Uriah would never be brought back to life. Forgiveness would not change those consequences. David finally had to realize that only God can put our past behind us. We can only create the mess; we cannot cover it. For that we must turn to the Lord our God.

A woman who had an abortion said she could not receive God's forgiveness because "nothing will ever bring my baby back to me." She had to learn, as David did, that we must turn around and receive pardon from God, even though the effects of our sin will continue.

What does it take to turn around? What does it take to change direction, to get back into fellowship with God where you belong?

TAKING THE ROAD BACK TO GOD

Psalm 51 is the cry of a man who finally has chosen to "come clean." David would never have turned to the Almighty unless he knew he would be received and welcomed back into fellowship. In his grief he rediscovered some of the attributes of God that gave him the assurance that the mess he created could be covered. He could take the road back. Those attributes include:

The Mercy of God

In the first verse he uses three different words to describe the mercy of God:

Be gracious to me, God, according to Your faithfulness;
According to the greatness of Your compassion, wipe out
my wrongdoings.
(Ps. 51:1 NASB)

To be *gracious* is to bestow a favor. David is asking God to give him something he does not deserve, something he has not earned. *Faithfulness* refers to "God's unfailing love." The Hebrew word has the same root as the word *stork,* a bird known for its tender care of its young. David pleads that God will not abandon him, but that He will carefully meet his deepest needs.

The third word, *compassion,* is related to the Hebrew word for *womb.* The imagery is of a mother tenderly nursing her newborn. David is saying, "God, please treat me tenderly because I am hurting; hold me gently in Your arms and take care of me."

Obviously, God now has David's complete attention, and David has God's attention, too. David is tired of traveling in the wrong direction and wants to come back to the warmth of the Father's house where he belongs.

How would David handle the fact that he destroyed so many lives? He made a statement in this prayer that we might be tempted to challenge. He says:

Against You, You only, I have sinned and done what is evil
in Your sight,
so that You are justified when You speak and blameless
when You judge.
(Ps. 51:4 NASB)

We might want to correct David here. He had sinned against
Bathsheba and Uriah, not to mention all his other wives to whom
he had pledged his allegiance. Why does he say his sin was against
God alone?

David understood full well that all sin is first and foremost a vio-
lation of the character of God. In the process of sinning against God
we happen to hurt other people; but it is with God we have to deal,
since it is His laws we have broken.

This is important to David for this reason: He knew he could
never be reconciled to those whom he had hurt on earth. He had
betrayed Bathsheba, and she might forgive him, but he could never
be restored to Uriah.

Sometimes sin causes human relationships to be so completely
severed that they can never be rectified on earth. Perhaps your father
died when you were a rebellious teenager. How you wish you could
have asked his forgiveness for the way you treated him! Or you may
have ruined a child's life through abuse, a lack of love, or a bad example. You might wish these things could be made right, but they
cannot be. What do you do?

David knew our first obligation is to be reconciled to the supreme lawgiver of the universe and then to commit all of our unfin-
ished business to Him. We recognize that He is completely just in His
dealings with us and in the lives of others we have wronged.

The Forgiveness of God

With a pencil, underline all the different terms in Psalm 51 David uses to refer to God's forgiveness. "Wipe out my wrongdoings." "Wash me thoroughly from my guilt." "Cleanse me from my sin." "Purify me." "Hide Your face from my sins." These are some of the expressions he uses to speak of what he wanted God to do in his heart.

Here was a man who knew both the power of sin and the praises of forgiveness. He believed his sordid past was not too much for God. He could be clean within his heart, where it really mattered.

When he prays, "Create in me a clean heart, God, and renew a steadfast spirit within me" (v. 10), he is counting on the ability of God to transform him within, despite the dreadful circumstances without. Once this miracle was done within, God would open David's lips so his mouth would declare God's praises.

Imagine! David could sing again! No doubt his wives were whispering in anger behind his back when he brought the new first lady Bathsheba into the king's palace. Think of the bitter gossip in David's army when word got out that he had one of his fifty mighty men deliberately killed to cover his adultery! News of the scandal flooded Jerusalem, with the story exaggerated each time it was told. David was the laugh of the town.

Yet, for all that, he would have his joy restored (v. 12), and he would teach other transgressors the way of God, and they would believe (v. 13). Yes, there was hope in the midst of the darkness.

The Providence of God

The mess David had made would not evaporate even though David had now received God's forgiveness. The bitter consequences would always be there—but God delights in bringing good out of evil. A rose would grow up with the thorns.

The Levitical law did not prescribe any sacrifice for the sins of murder and adultery. The law specified that the offender was to die. This is why David prayed:

> For You do not delight in sacrifice, otherwise I would give it;
> You do not take pleasure in burnt offering.
> The sacrifices of God are a broken spirit;
> A broken and a contrite heart, God, You will not despise.
> (Ps. 51:16–17 NASB)

God would not despise that broken and contrite heart. Out of the ashes, some blessing would come.

After Bathsheba became David's wife, the child that was conceived in a sinful act died. David had other children with her, though, and the best known was Solomon.

Strictly speaking, Solomon should never have been born, for Bathsheba should never have become one of David's wives. Yet God is never at a loss in the midst of the wreckage of human failure and sin. God told David that Solomon would be great and would be a special blessing to the people (2 Sam. 12:24–25; 1 Kings 1:37). Unfortunately, Solomon had two hearts—one to love God and another to love women and wealth. Through it all, however, (1) he built the temple that David had wanted to build for God, (2) he wrote thousands of proverbs that became a part of the Word of God, and (3) both he and his mother Bathsheba are listed in the genealogy of Christ found in Matthew 1:6.

Do you recall the story of the beautiful piece of cloth on which some ink had accidentally been spilled? Though the ink could not be removed, an artist painted a picture on it and used the blotch as part of the scenery.

God has had much experience in using our sins to create beauty and value. Indeed, out of the greatest failure of mankind (the sin of

Adam and Eve), God brought the greatest display of His mercy and grace in redemption.

REASONS TO TURN AROUND

Let's summarize some lessons David learned. If we have wandered from the path of fellowship, we shall be encouraged to turn around and become fruitful for God once more.

It Is Never Too Late to Turn to God

It may be harder now than it was in the past, but it is never too late. The time is always appropriate to do what is right. As long as you are alive, you still have the capacity to turn around and head in a different direction.

Though our sin may have caused irreparable damage, we should turn to God in repentance and faith. Only He can make the best of the mess.

When we were lost in the winter storm in northern Wisconsin, we looked for a crossroads where we could turn around. God has provided such a place on the road of life. The cross of Christ is the point at which we can reverse our direction and walk in the direction of God. That cross is a reminder that we can turn around.

David lived before the cross, so he did not see God's forgiveness with the clarity we do—but even his sin was eventually laid on Christ. Yes, God says, "Turn around."

God Can Put Your Past Behind You

What about the memories of our sin? What about the ruts left in the snow? How can we ever be free from the reminders of our failure?

A businessman was notorious for saving everything. His office files were bulging with useless papers he would never look at. His exasperated secretary kept asking him if she could dispose of all the old, useless material. The man was reluctant, but she insisted. "All right," he finally said, "but be sure you photocopy everything before you throw it away!"

When God cleans out your life, He doesn't make photocopies; we do. He just throws the files away. Once our sins are blotted out and cast into the depths of the sea, we can move forward—in the direction of God. Why should we remember what God has promised to forget? As already emphasized, we must leave the consequences to God. When we have done all we can to repair the damage, God must do the rest. We do the possible; God does the impossible.

God Wants You to Look Ahead

He wants you to look through the windshield rather than into the rearview mirror. Once the direction of your life has changed, there is no use in looking back to a past you have left behind.

It is more important to see where you are going than to be preoccupied with where you have been.

David knew what it was like to slide into the ditch along the path of life, but God lifted him to his feet and set him on the right course:

> He drew me up from the pit of destruction,
> out of the miry bog,
> and set my feet upon a rock,
> making my steps secure.
> He put a new song in my mouth,
> a song of praise to our God.
> Many will see and fear,
> and put their trust in the LORD.
> (Ps. 40:2–3)

Once you have been lifted out of the ditch and set back onto the right road, there is little value in living in the past. God wants to put your past behind you so you can continue living the rest of your days for His glory.

ACTION STEP

Learn the lesson of waiting on God. Bow in submission without any specific agenda except to meditate on the Scriptures, that you might be refreshed in God's presence.

Set specific spiritual goals for the future. List character qualities you want God to develop within you. Target specific areas of change in your personal disciplines and relationships with others.

Make all the changes in your life you would make if you knew you had exactly one more year to live.

Turn from every sinful act or attitude that God brings to your mind. Let such an affirmation become a part of your daily walk with God.

Notes

1. Faith L. Mischler, "Reproof," *Watchman-Examiner* (Vol. 47 1959).

2. Louisa Fletcher Tarkington, "The Land of Beginning Again" in *The Land of Beginning Again*, ed. Frederick F. Shannon (Revell, 1921), 8.

3. "Children's Living Arrangements, US Census, November 14, 2023, https://www.census.gov/library/visualizations/interactive/childrens-living-arrangements.html.

4. "Devastatingly Pervasive: 1 in 3 Women Globally Experience Violence," World Health Organization, March 9, 2021, https://www.who.int/news/item/09-03-2021-devastatingly-pervasive-1-in-3-women-globally-experience-violence.

5. Augustine, *The Confessions of Saint Augustine*, Book 6, Chapter 10.

6. Robert Fulghum, *All I Really Need to Know I Learned in Kindergarten: Uncommon Thoughts on Common Things* (Villard Books, 1988), 56–58.

7. Guy Condon, "Fatherhood Aborted," *Christianity Today*, December 9, 1996, 37.

8. William G. Justice, *Guilt and Forgiveness* (Baker, 1980), 105.

9. Ibid., 95.

10. Cheryl Lavin, "Guilty of Adultery," *Chicago Tribune*, September 13, 1989, Section 5, 1.

11. Richard Brzeczek et al., *Addicted to Adultery: How We Saved Our Marriage/How You Can Save Yours* (Bantam, 1989), 36.

12. Lavin, "Guilty of Adultery," 1.

13. Ibid.

14. Brzeczek, *Addicted to Adultery*, 49.

15. Lavin, "Guilty of Adultery," 1.

16. Patrick Carnes, *Out of the Shadows: Understanding Sexual Addiction* (CompCare, 1985), 64.

---

17. Keith Miller, *Sin: Overcoming the Ultimate Deadly Addiction* (Harper & Row, 1987), 52.

18. Ann Landers, "Silence Can Be Deadly in Sexual Abuse Cases," *Chicago Tribune*, October 30, 1989, Section 5, 3. Permission granted by Ann Landers and Creators Syndicate.

19. "Child Sexual Abuse Statistics," National Center for Victims of Crime, https://victimsofcrime.org/child-sexual-abuse-statistics. The same study found that one in twenty boys will be a victim of sexual abuse.

20. David Seamands, *The Healing of Memories* (Victor Books, 1985), 8.

21. P. Roger Hillerstrom, *Intimate Deception* (Multnomah, 1989), 30.

22. Michael Castleman, "Addicted to Love," *Chicago Tribune,* January 30, 1991, 6.

23. Augustus Toplady, "Rock of Ages" (1776).

24. Anne R. Cousin, "O Christ, What Burdens Bowed Thy Head" (1871).

25. L. Gregory Jones, *Embodying Forgiveness* (Eerdmans, 1995), 6.

26. Ibid., 4.

27. C. S. Lewis, *Mere Christianity* (McMillan, 1952), 204.

28. S. I. McMillen, *None of These Diseases* (Revell, 1972), 54.

29. Mark Bubeck, *The Adversary* (Moody Publishers, 1975), 74.

30. Ibid., 106–9.

Honest discussions about our earthly lives— and of our glorious, eternal ones.

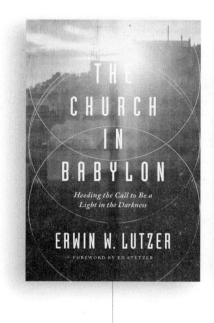

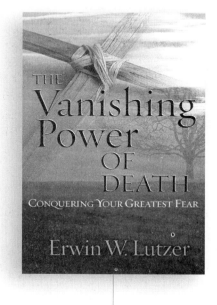

Dr. Lutzer will walk you through the many parallels between the church in America and God's people in Babylon. Then he'll explain what we can learn from the Israelites about maintaining our faith in the midst of a pagan culture.

When the tomb was found empty, death lost its power. Consider the evidence for the resurrection and its impact on the disciples. Sure to invigorate your faith and make a life-changing difference.

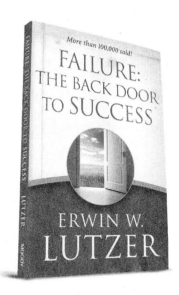

Find the good in your failure

Speaking to one of our most common struggles, *Failure: The Back Door to Success* shows us how God uses even our shortcomings in His perfect plan. When we know that God is the one at work in us, we can take comfort amid disappointment and live each day with great expectation.

Also available as an eBook

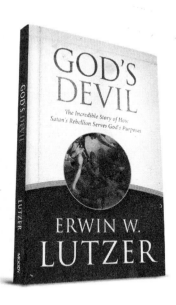

"It is the best treatment of the person and work of the enemy I have ever read."

—R. C. Sproul, from the foreword

An intriguing overview of Satan's career: his fall, work, and demise.

Also available as an eBook

MOODY
Publishers

From the Word to Life